This book is dedicated to Peter Steiger and Esther Schoellkopf-Steiger.

This publication was made possible with the kind support of
Belacqua Immoblien AG, Herrliberg

Marianne Burkhalter, Christian Sumi

The Steiger House Doldertal, Zurich 1959

Rudolf Steiger and Flora Steiger-Crawford

With current photos by Leonardo Finotti

“Dreaming Spaces”

“Is it raining?” visitors ask. “No, it’s sunny.”
The sound of the rushing water from the creek nearby is disorienting.

We sit in the middle of the room and look out into the forest. As if it were a brightly lit theater curtain, the scene changing with the four seasons, morphing into a spectacle of whiteness in winter and dark green ancient woodland in summer. The colors are reflected in the interior, influencing the moods of those who live here. Rainy days are cozy and introverted, sunny days are expressive and thrillingly beautiful. Our view, a large image, a single space, merging almost seamlessly with the surroundings. A symbiotic interplay between nature and architecture. A monumental facade from the outside, a room with a stunning backdrop from the inside.

“How do you sleep here?”

Where is the bed, where is the wardrobe, where is the dining table and the sofa by the TV? Rooms without any specific functionality, without any specific purpose. An empty center, a central space that unburdens the other two wings. Unusable, unused, free to be appropriated; children take possession of the space, holistically defined, beyond the space, without boundaries, determined not by the enclosed space, but by the children’s play.

“How do you live without doors?”

Doors protect us, delimit us, safeguard our privacy. You on one side, me on the other. That’s where I’m at home. Doors close off a room, doors fragment the space, impede the spatial flow. We slide our doors open and closed every day. There is something liberating about modifiable dynamic space.

“Where is the shower?”

No doors inside, but doors in the stairwell, where nobody expects them. Four possible entrances, to the kitchen, to the shower, to the living room, to the private room. Is the house a socially minded, flexible house? A home for multiple generations in modern times?

It is interesting how life and perception are changed by open spaces. Peter Steiger and his wife, Esther, told us a great deal about his parents’ free spirit and their social life. They built a house that made modern living possible, thus anticipating a current postulate of contemporary floor-plan typologies.

This book is based on the drawings and photos that Peter Steiger made available to us (now in the archives of the gta Institute – ETH Zurich). Peter Steiger recognizes the characteristic imprimatur of his mother, Flora Steiger-Crawford, in the first surviving drawing. We would like to thank him and Esther Schoellkopf-Steiger for all the inspiring, interesting conversations and dedicate this book to the two of them.

Marianne Burkhalter and Christian Sumi, Doldertal, summer 2024

Site and House

Photos by Leonardo Finotti

Brazilian architect and photographer Leonardo Finotti took three sessions – in 2018, 2021 and 2023 – to photograph the house. The images loosely form the backbone of the book. Finotti's many achievements include his comprehensive photographic documentation of Brazilian modernism. This photographic material underpins the systematic recording of this "architecture of the century." Finotti's work is informed by his training as an architect, which is the basis of his in-depth and precise view, as well as the questions he poses about what he finds. Working with his wife, Michelle Jean de Castro, Finotti repeatedly creates exhibitions and catalogs, setting his photographs within a broader framework – nature, the city, the social context. His approach is always documentary, methodically political.

These are image constructions, constructed images. Photographs do not depict reality "as it is," but are a constructed vision of reality. In his publications, as here, the photos are usually printed as double-spreads and offer three viewing options: looking at the individual image on the left, on the right or considering the photo in its entirety. A cardboard cover is included with the book *Brazilian Cities*.[1] This strategy recalls the fold-out landscape images, overlays and masks in the Red Books by the great landscape architect Humphry Repton. His perspectives portray the landscape on the one hand after the intervention, with the overlay section closed, as well as before the intervention, when the image is unfolded.[2]

1— See Leonardo Finotti, *Brazilian Cities*, Santos, São Paulo, Editora Brasileira de Arte e Cultura, 2023.

2— See Stephen Daniels, *Humphry Repton. Landscape Gardening and the Geography of Georgian England*, New Haven et al., Yale University Press, 1999.

Dieter Kienast

Almost in the Forest

In almost all of the gardens we plan, we don't have to start from scratch. There is always "something there" already: one time it is a striking tree, a topography full of suspense, a nice view; the next time we find an existing garden that does not meet the approval of its owners. It is our proclaimed goal to create a "good garden" with as few operations as possible. The few operations are not based, however, on a consciously ascetic attitude. Moreover, it is the realization that most places do not allow a large scale of themes and elements due to their size or their limitations without having an overloaded effect.

This garden's main theme is the development of a precise topography. Our small garden consists of many small parts which are arranged around the remarkable '50s building on various levels in the terrain. Erected by Rudolf Steiger and Flora Steiger-Crawford, the famous architect couple, the post and beam house is oriented towards the steep slope by the valley with the brook with an impressive old forest. The forest is omnipresent in the inside of the building as well as the various garden parts and only towards the west does one have a view of the neighboring building, the city and the lake. The goal of the architectural garden intervention is the different phrasing of the partial gardens which are separated into three sections due to their situation in the terrain, or with reference to the building: the steep slope from the walkway to the entrance, the east and west side garden to the first living floor and the garden to the second floor. The hedge on the western border is determined to be a summary and connection of the three garden parts. It follows the terrain and has a height of 2.20 meters. It has been conceived as a mixed trimmed hedge whose composition of species corresponds to that of the adjoining forest: Fagus, Carpinus, Acer, Viburnum, Crataegus, etc. Thus, the hedge represents an extract of the forest in the controlled form of a garden. The stepped levels of the slope in the form of walls and steep inclines are accentuated with unified Tilia and Taxus hedges planted in front.

Along the walkway a double hedge of white flowering Chaenomeles and Ligustrum (privet) forms the termination and base of the steeply rising hill which is planted with ivy and fern and has a small vegetable garden incorporated into it. On the east side of the first floor we find the large gravel square which, being located directly outside the kitchen, is perfectly suitable as a place for having breakfast. The west garden is three steps lower and consists of a wide lawn surface with sculpturally trimmed box.

The largest of the small garden sections is assigned to the second floor. Originally it was a slanted part with a small and all-too-modest limestone wall as a lower termination point. When it was contrived, the relationship to the garden style of the '30s and '40s was clear, but it hardly corresponded to the powerful clarity of the architecture.

By raising the termination wall in the front and leveling off the slope in the back, a horizontal level is being introduced which seems to adjoin the forest. The edge of the garden is framed with a small water basin. The wide garden level finds a precise termination in the change of material, from gravel to water which, at the same time, continues to guide the view further on. Cut into the gravel lies a rectangular, lowered piece of lawn – similar to a green carpet – which enhances the sloped lines of the garden section with its clear geometry. In the springtime, the geometrically planted Narcissus redraw the lawn rectangle. During the course of the year, the strictness of the plantings is relieved by more liberated groupings of plants. Sitting on the bench, we recognize to our left the terrace with its glorious Cornus kousa. Directly in front of us is the piece of lawn with the young Cornus – enhancing the asymmetry – and the rusty reel line of the water basin where the adjoining forest, which seems almost directly wedded to the garden, is fragmentarily reflected. Closeness and distance of the built and grown world condense into a place which is simultaneously full of tension and calm.[3]

[3] — Excerpt from: Dieter Kienast, *Gärten. Gardens.* Basel, Birkhäuser, 1997, pp. 146–151. Translated from German by Bruce Almberg and Katja Steiner.

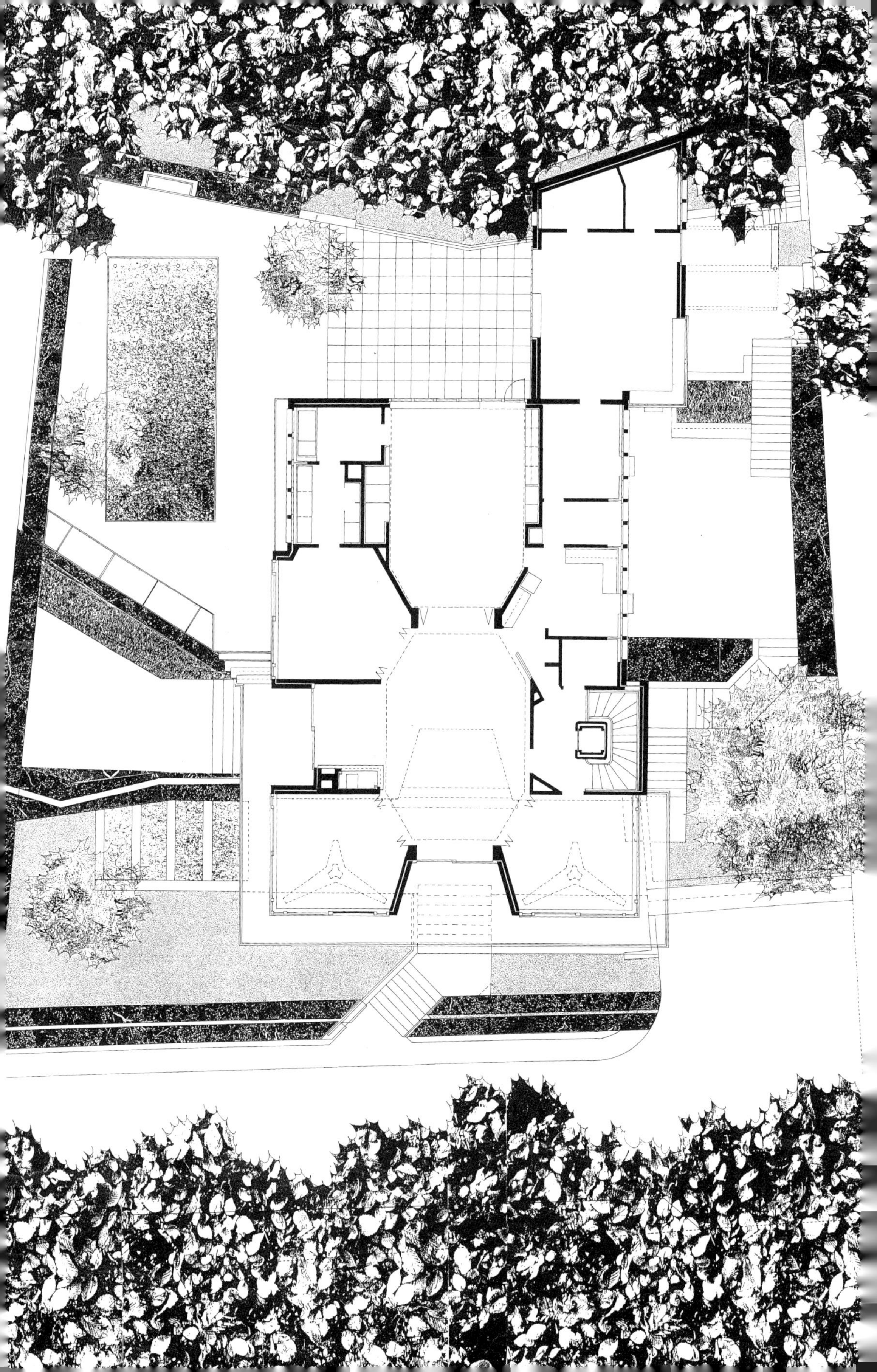

Photo by: Georg Aerni

Living in the Valley

Zurich A number of valleys define the area surrounding Zurich, the Erlenbacher Tobel, the Küsnachter Tobel, the Wehrenbachtobel and the Wolfbachtobel on the right side of the lake, the area known as the Doldertal. That is where Swiss architectural theorist Sigfried Giedion, known for his groundbreaking book *Space, Time and Architecture*,[4] a milestone in the historiography of modernism, chose to live. In 1936, he also became the client for the two Doldertal houses by Alfred and Emil Roth with Marcel Breuer.[5] In 1960/61, Alfred Roth's Fellowship Home was built on the opposite side, immediately adjacent to the Steiger House by Rudolf Steiger and Flora Steiger-Crawford.

Küsnacht A residential building by architect Fred Cramer (1923–2018) can be found on the Küsnachter Tobel, just above the creek (Rüsselbach/Dorfbach). The house in exposed concrete is part of a larger ensemble. Its horizontal orientation in the landscape makes it particularly striking, as does the way in which it intermeshes with the exterior and references later buildings by Marcel Breuer in Switzerland, such as the Staehelin House in Feldmeilen (1958) and the Koerfer House in Moscia in Ticino (1966).[6] Architect Ernst Gisel's home and the studio house of Max Bill, architect, painter, sculptor, and founder of the Hochschule für Gestaltung (Ulm School of Design) are also located nearby.[7]

Los Angeles In the early 1950s, John Entenza launched the Case Study Houses program on the US West Coast and offered an entire generation a highly regarded platform for their talents.[8] The program combined two themes: prefabrication and the question of modern, alternative forms of housing. In this context, Craig Ellwood, one of the most important architects from the younger generation,[9] "transposed" Mies van der Rohe's steel buildings into the world of industrial construction. Unlike Mies, he did not use sharp-edged, square HEA profiles, but opted instead for rounded IPE industrial profiles. The construction sites are often in canyon-like valleys in Los Angeles' hinterland. With his Bridge House (1968), Ellwood adopted a more radical take on the theme and set the building across the river in the form of an architectural Vierendeel truss: "in the ravine"[10] and not "on the ravine" like the Steiger House.

São Paulo In 1950, Italian architect Lina Bo Bardi built a home for herself, Casa de Vidro (Glass House), in the dense jungle on the outskirts of São Paulo.[11] The front-facing, open living area is on stilts and is accessed via a simple double staircase that runs "under and through the house." The intermediate landing offers an initial vista looking "back" into the landscape. A patio lets light into the entrance area, while the living and ancillary rooms are set in a sequence, positioned one after the other on the hillside. The essential character of the Steiger House and the Casa de Vidro could not be more different. The driveway under the house (Le Corbusier, Villa Savoye) and the fragile stilts contrast with the two monumental struts in the Steiger House's vestibule. In addition, Lina Bo Bardi's rather neutral living space contrasts with the Steiger House's strict classical typology, dividing up spaces according to their function.

All these examples share a dream, a wish to live close to the city but within nature, in a quest to find new, open living spaces and alternative forms of living – a typical theme of modernity.

4 — Sigfried Giedion, *Space, Time and Architecture. The Growth of a New Tradition*, Cambridge, Harvard University Press, 1941. See also, anticipating various themes of *Space, Time and Architecture* the publication of the book project: *The Origin of Modern Man. An Unfinished Book Project, 1929–1938*, eds. Sokratis Georgiadis and Almut Grunewald, Zurich, gta Verlag, 2023.

5 — Cf. on this point Arthur Rüegg, *Die Doldertalhäuser. Ein Hauptwerk des Neuen Bauens in Zürich*, with essays by Alfred Roth and Andres Giedion, exhib. cat., ETH Hönggerberg, HIL, Architekturfoyer, Zurich, gta Verlag, 1996.

6 — See in addition Marcel Breuer. "Marcel Breuer. Casas americanas / American Houses," *2G*, 17, texts by Antonio Armesto, Marcel Breuer et al., Barcelona, Gili, 2001.

7 — Cf. on this point "Max Bill. Arquitecto / Architect," *2G*, 29/30, texts by Karin Gimmi, Stanislaus von Moos et al., Barcelona, Gili, 2004.

8 — Cf. on this point Elisabeth A. T. Smith, *Case Study Houses*, ed. Peter Goessel, Cologne, Taschen, 2002.

9 — Cf. on this point "Craig Ellwood. 15 casas / 15 Houses," *2G*, 12, texts by Livio Vacchini, Norman Foster et al, Barcelona, Gili, 1999. Like the Steiger House, the Smith House (1958) is also on a steep slope.

10 — The view through the transparent house is reminiscent of the collage of the Resor House (1938) by Mies van der Rohe. This shows the view from the living space into the landscape towards the mountains. In the Steiger House, the view into the gorge is not a central theme. The images concentrate on the interior of the house, with the gorge and the trees becoming a two-dimensional backdrop, a flat background.

11 — Cf. on this point "Lina Bo Bardi. Obra construida / Built work," *2G*, 23/24, texts by Olivia de Oliveira, Barcelona, Gili, 2002.

Topography

Site and Terrain Sections

The laboriously constructed private road with its own street lighting and the Steiger House (1959) are the driving forces behind Wolfbachtobel's urbanization.[12] On plans drawn up by the engineers Fietz & Hauri, the massive displacement/removal of terrain is shown in yellow and areas where earth was added in red. Set close to the road on the slope, the Steiger House (A) leaves its mark on the streetscape. Architecture and thoroughfare exert a reciprocal influence one upon the other. The asymmetrical design is shaped by the irregular, undulating terrain, while the different heights of the landscape on both sides of the building snugly accommodate the two-story east-facing utility section.

Alfred Roth's Fellowship Home (1961) (B) is set back from the road. Positioned in a topographical depression, it "shrinks back" from the valley. The Doldertal houses (1936) on the other side "turn away from the valley" and are staggered along the access road to the southeast.

12 — Cf. on the topic of the valley, Matthias Senn, "Historisches zu Zürichs Wolfbach," in: *Altstadt Kurier*, April 2012.

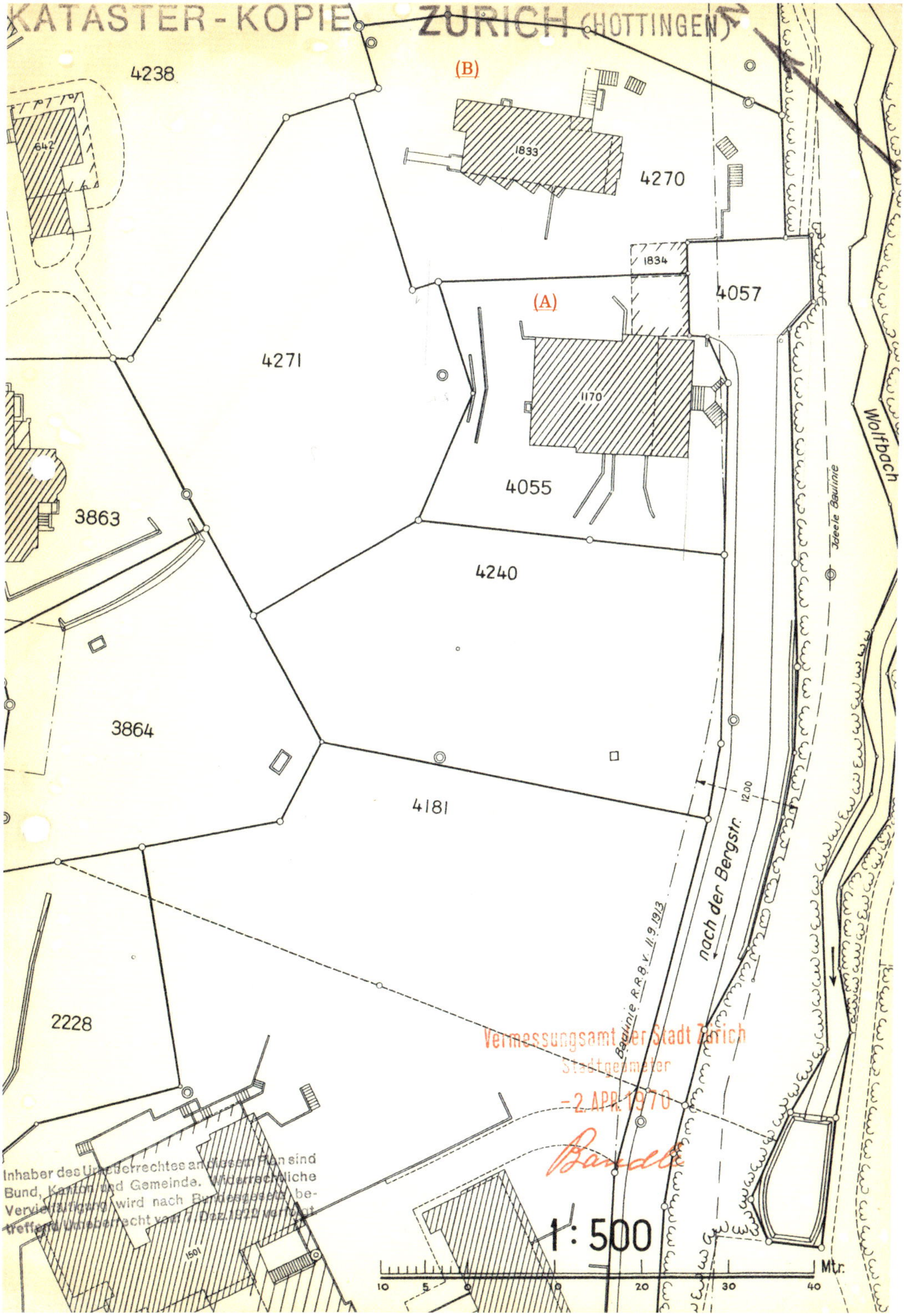

KATASTER-KOPIE ZÜRICH (HOTTINGEN)
(B)
(A)
4238
642
1833
4270
1834
4057
4271
1170
4055
3863
4240
Wolfbach
Ideele Baulinie
3864
4181
12.00
nach der Bergstr.
Baulinie R.R.B.v. 11.9.1913
2228
1501
Vermessungsamt der Stadt Zürich
Stadtgeometer
-2. APR. 1970
Inhaber des Urheberrechtes an diesem Plan sind Bund, Kanton und Gemeinde. Widerrechtliche Vervielfältigung wird nach Bundesgesetz betreffend Urheberrecht vom 7. Dez. 1922 verfolgt.
1:500
10 5 0 10 20 30 40 Mtr.

Tel. 24 67 50 Herr Prof.

1. Situation grösserer Masstab ?
2. Kurvenplan " " ?
3. " " mehr!

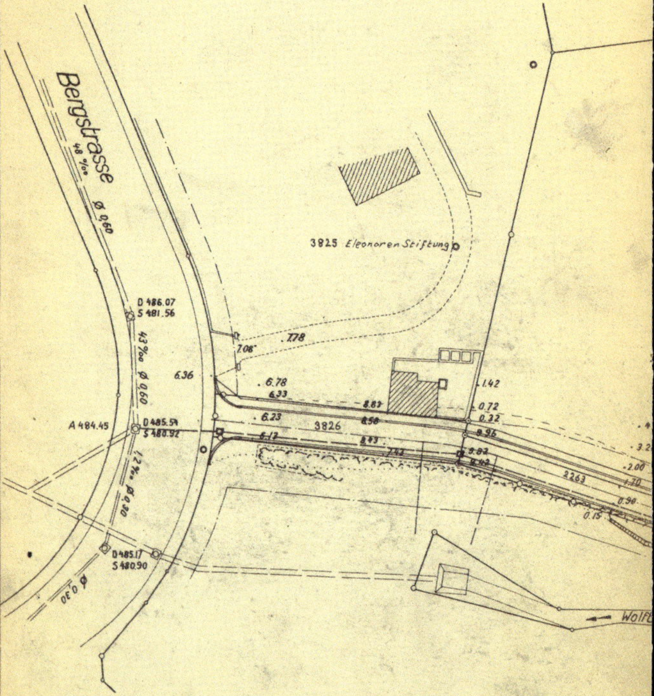

DR. R. STEIGER
BÜRO: M. E. HAEFELI, W. M. MOSER, DR. R. STEIGER

HAUS STEIGER mit Wolfbachtobel

173	1:500	6.10.58 ms

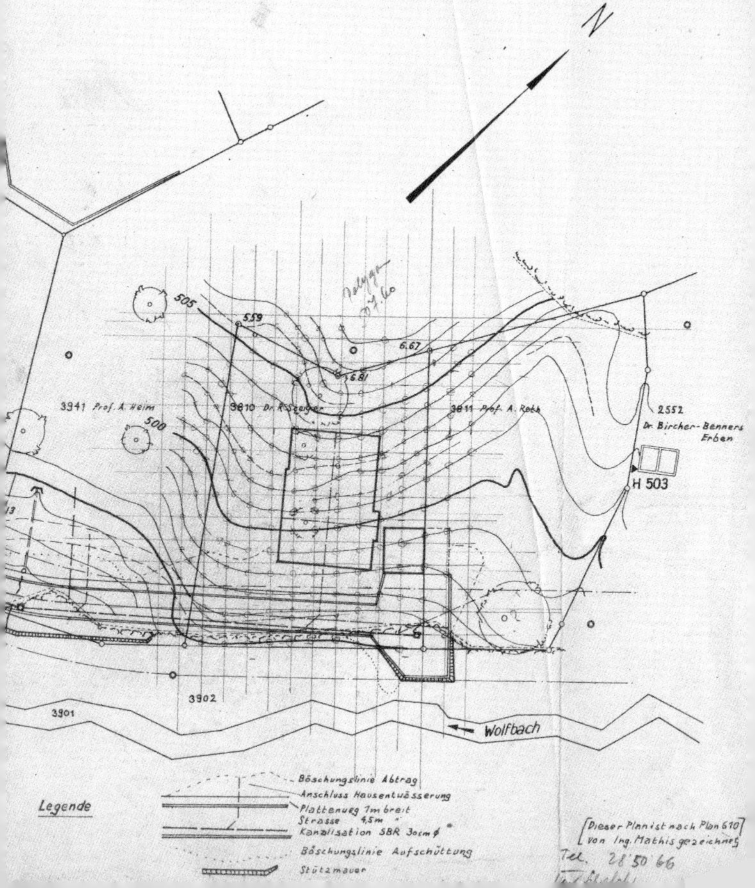
N
505
559
6.67
500
3941 Prof. A. Heim
3811 Prof. A. Roth
2552
Dr. Bircher-Benners Erben
H 503
3902
3901
Wolfbach
Legende
Böschungslinie Abtrag
Anschluss Hausentwässerung
Plattenweg 1m breit
Strasse 4,5m
Kanalisation SBR 30cm ø
Böschungslinie Aufschüttung
Stützmauer
Dieser Plan ist nach Plan 610 von Ing. Mathis gezeichnet
Tel. 28 50 66

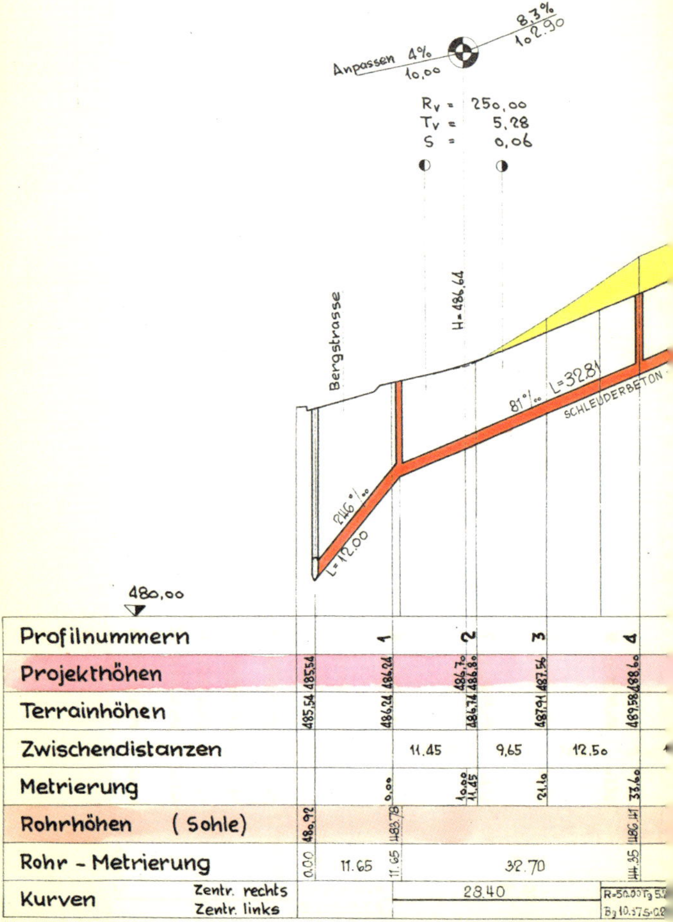

Anpassen 4%
10,00
8,3%
102.90
Rv = 250,00
Tv = 5,28
S = 0,06
Bergstrasse
H= 486,64
81‰ L=32.81
SCHLEUDERBETON
246‰
L=12.00
480,00
Profilnummern
Projekthöhen
Terrainhöhen
Zwischendistanzen
Metrierung
Rohrhöhen (Sohle)
Rohr - Metrierung
Kurven
Zentr. rechts
Zentr. links
1
2
3
4
485,54 485,54
486,24 486,24
486,70 486,80
486,74
487,91 487,56
489,58 488,60
11.45
9,65
12.50
0.00
10,00 11,45
21,10
33,60
480,92
483.78
486.41
0.00
11.65
11.65
32.70
44.35
28.40

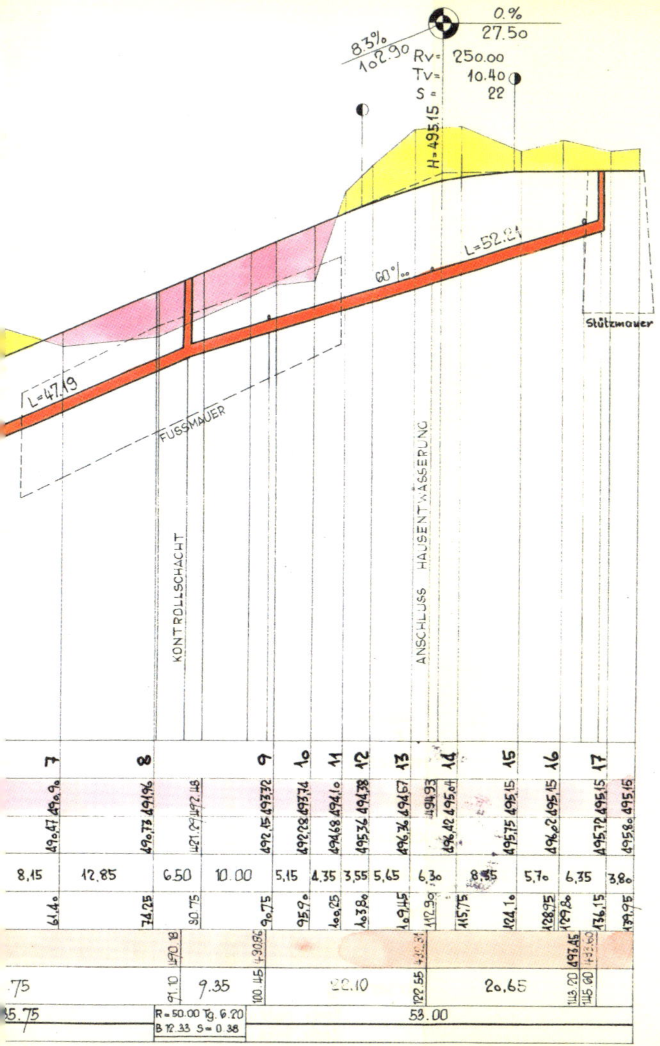

0.%
27.50
8.3%
102.90
Rv= 250.00
Tv= 10.40
S = 22
H=495.15
L=52.21
60‰
Stützmauer
L=47.19
FUSSMAUER
KONTROLLSCHACHT
ANSCHLUSS HAUSENTWÄSSERUNG
7
8
9
10
11
12
13
14
15
16
17
R=50.00 Tg. 6.20
B 12.33 S=0.38
53.00

BAUHERRSCHAFT

Zufahrt zum Wolfbachtobel

Querprofile

unter Vorbehalt
Genehmigt durch
Verfügung des Bauvorstandes I
Nr. 129 vom 9. Apr. 1959

KOPIE		2. 2. 59 dR	FIETZ & HAURI
PLAN Nº	MASSTAB		Dipl. Bauingenieure
58 14 04	1:100		ZÜRICH 1, Bahnhofstr. 24

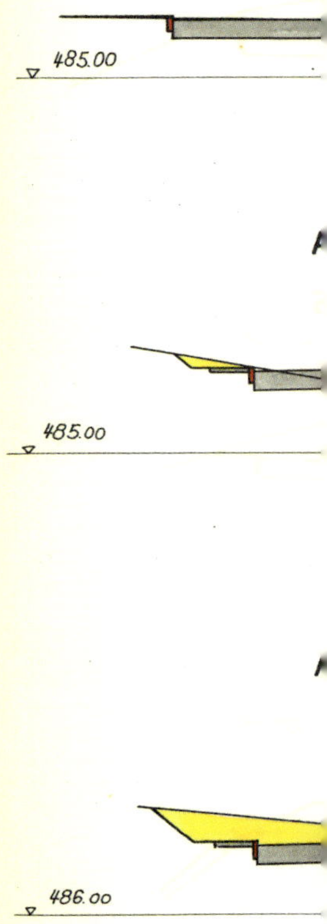

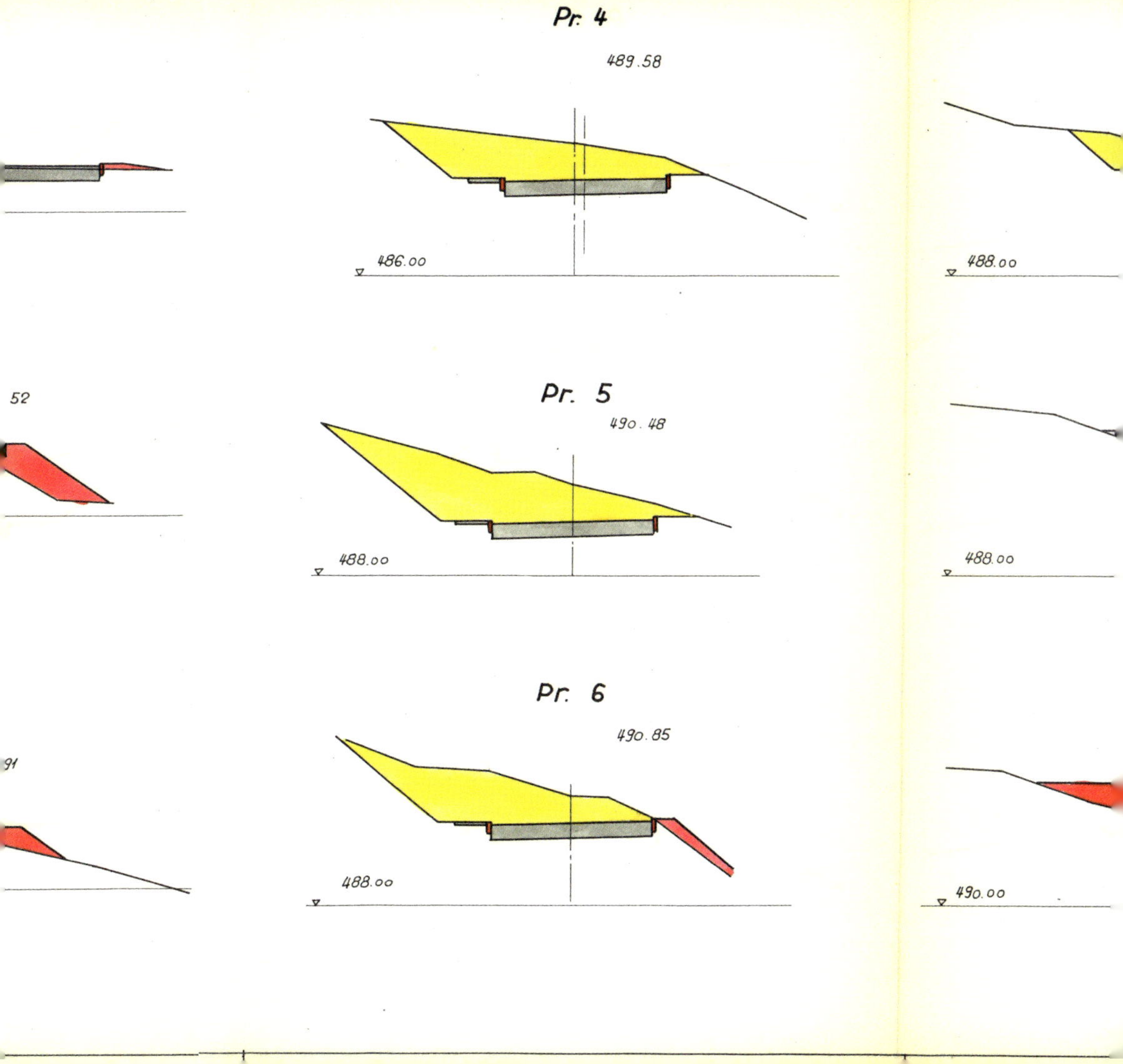
Pr. 4
489.58
486.00
488.00
52
Pr. 5
490. 48
488.00
488.00
91
Pr. 6
490. 85
488.00
490.00

Pr. 7

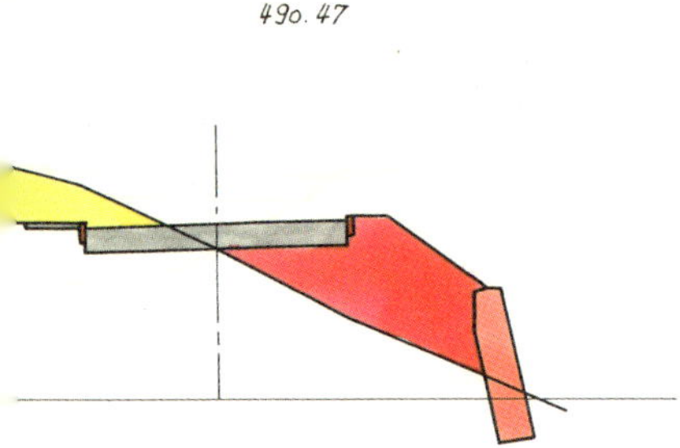

Pr. 8

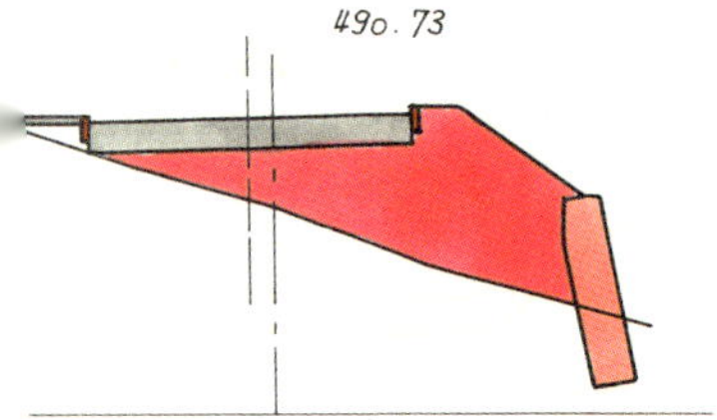

Pr. 9

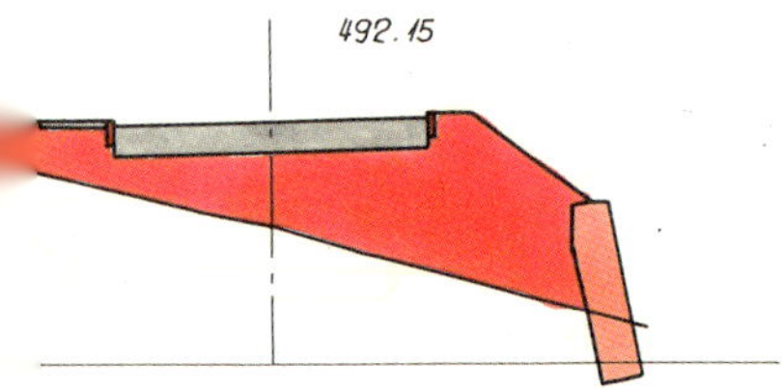

Pr. 10

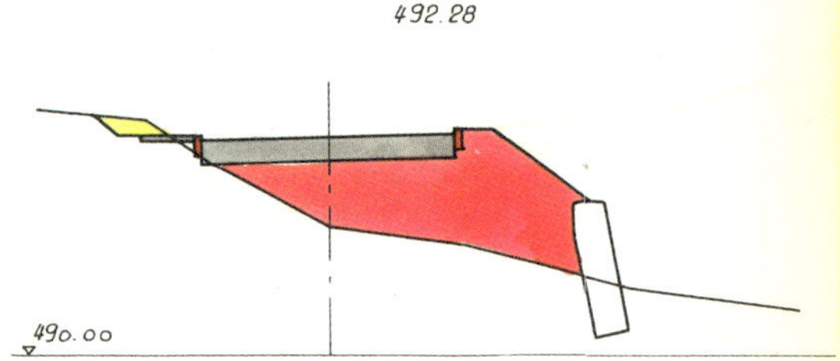

Pr. 11

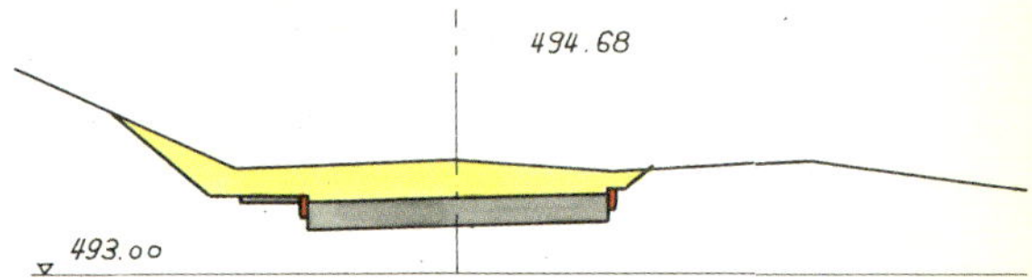

Pr. 12

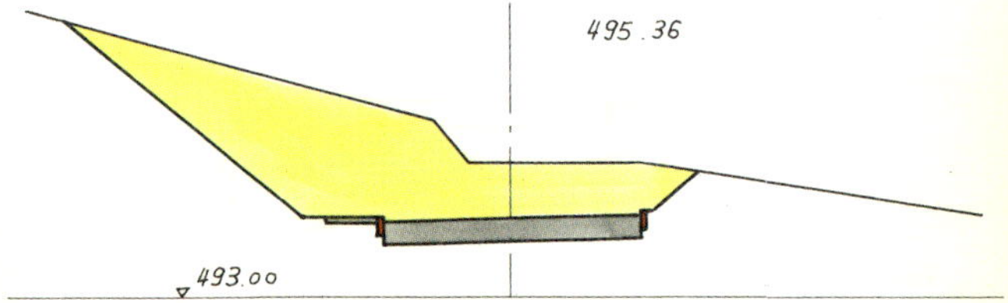

Pr. 13

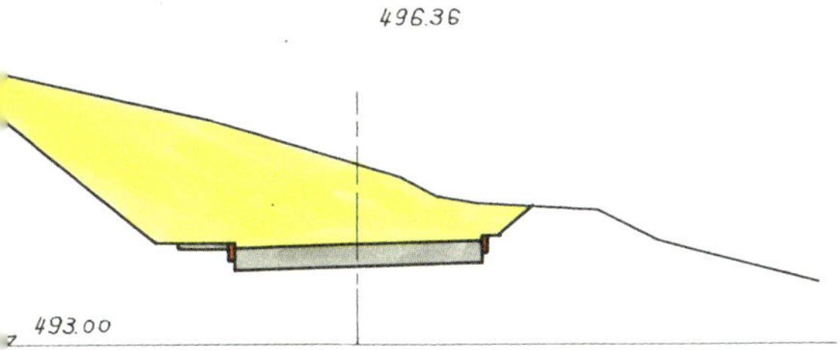

Pr. 14

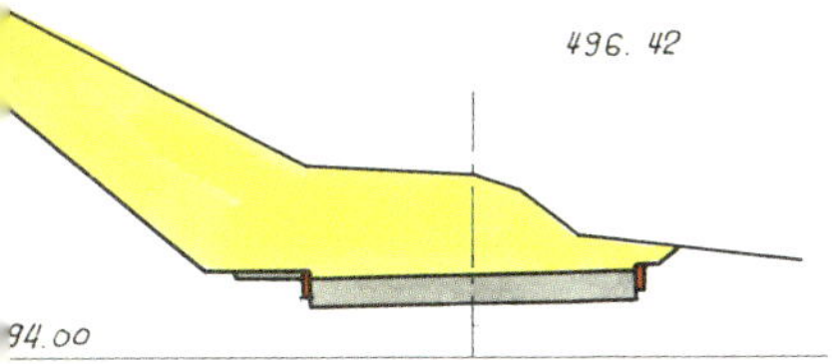

Pr. 15

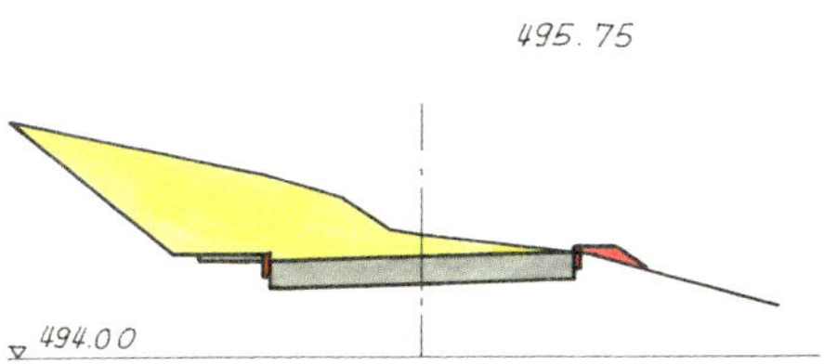

Pr. 16

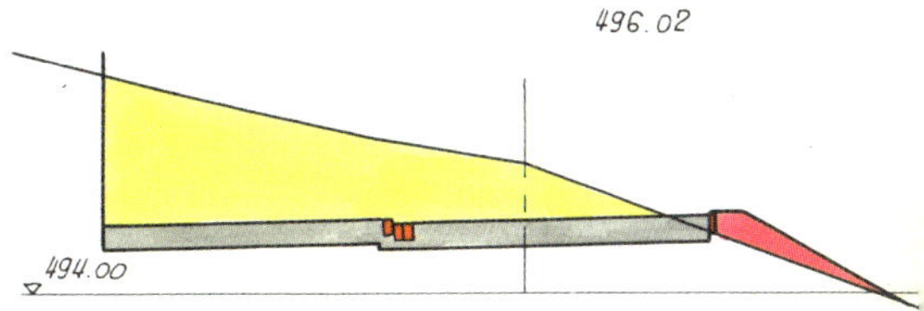

Pr. 17

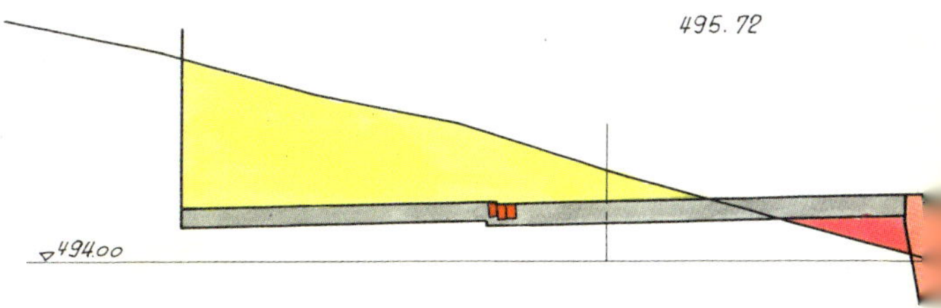

Chronology

Plans 1956–1958

A concise reconstruction of the chronology based on the extant plans[13] of the Steiger House reveals how the floor plan and section gradually grew more specific over a two-year period. As well as addressing geometric simplifications, for instance straightening certain sections and adjusting the size of the corner rooms, variants study how the staircase and the kitchen are arranged in relation to the central space. A solution with rear access from Belsitostrasse situated above the Steiger House, and the option of a split-level typology were also explored. The fireplace, moved around to different positions in the various iterations, proved tricky to incorporate, pointing to the interior design challenge posed by the central room. Nevertheless, the concept of the central space that featured in Flora Steiger-Crawford's first hand-drawn plans is essentially retained throughout.

The essential design elements are already apparent in the first plan for the Steiger House: a large, hexagonal central space with a series of skylights running around on the top of the space and three rooms incorporating corner glazing docked in a radial configuration around it, with recessed terraces set between them, as well as a cantilevered slab around the circumference. Flora Steiger-Crawford's studio adjoins the building on the hillside.[14]

The floor plans (No. 33 and No. 34) are signed "fs," referring to Flora Steiger-Crawford. The couple's son, Peter Steiger, has noted that the rhythm of the drawn lines clearly reveals his mother's signature style. That suggests she played a key role as an architect in conceiving the house. Most of the later plans bear the letters "ms," the contracted form used by Martin Steiger, Peter Steiger's younger brother.

Perspective View No. 35, undated

View with garages on the west side.
The supporting slabs with projecting sections for the entrance are located under the upper, radially arranged wall slabs. (Author unknown)

13 — We do not know to what extent there were other variants, especially between the points in time indicated here. The chronology is based on the available material and makes no claim to be exhaustive. The following pages show a selection of plans made for the Steiger House.

14 — Flora Steiger-Crawford worked primarily as a sculptor from 1938 onwards, see *Flora Steiger-Crawford 1899–1991*, ed. ETH Zurich, Department of Architecture, Zurich, gta Verlag, 2003.

Plans No. 29–35

June 20 / 26, 1956

Upper apartment

Three rooms and the kitchen, between them two loggias looking south and west, the staircase facing east, and the passageway to the rear-facing studio, behind the kitchen the maid's room. The studio protrudes from the rear facade.

Lower apartment

A small kitchen and bathroom are provided in the room to the rear on the west side. The area for the sculptures is placed under the studio and is implemented like this in the final project too. The entrance sinks into the terrain; slabs support the table structure of the second story.

The fundamental concept is already clear in Flora Steiger-Crawford's hand-drawn plans no. 33 and 34: a central room with the other rooms configured "radially" around it; no real balcony yet, just a cantilevered slab, an elevator between the staircase and kitchen, the fireplace on the side of the staircase.

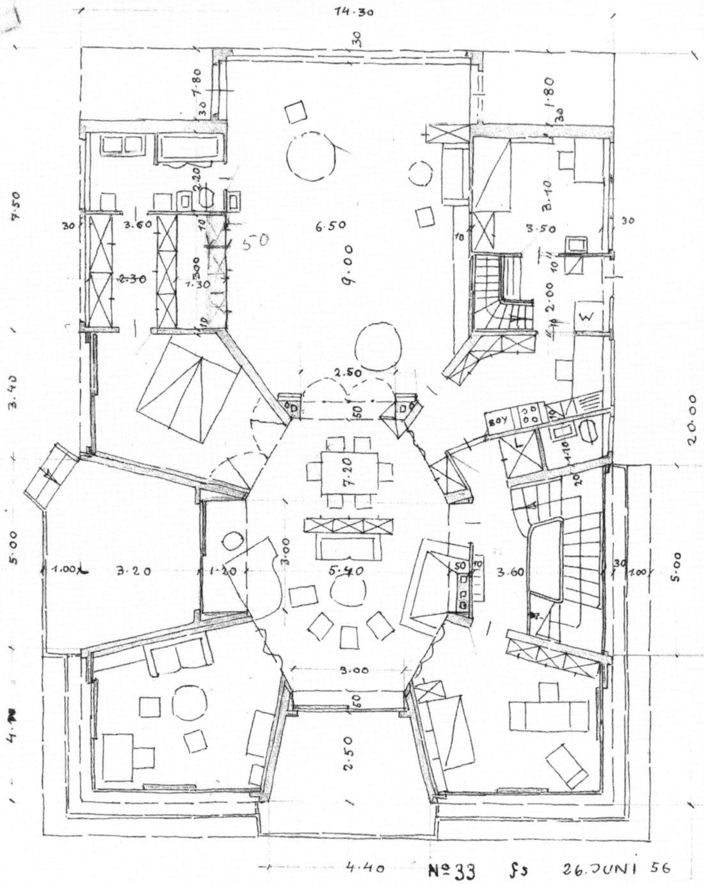

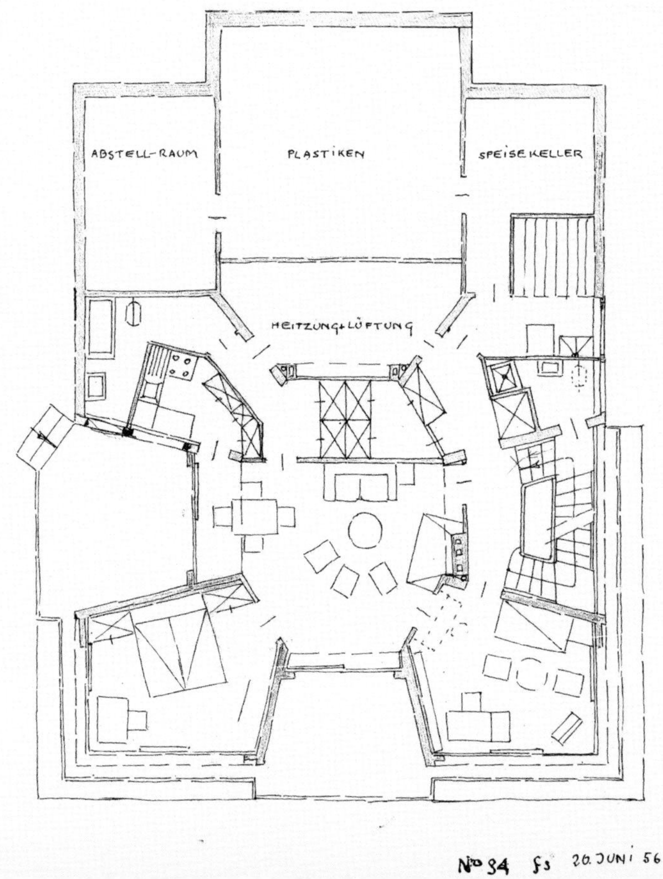

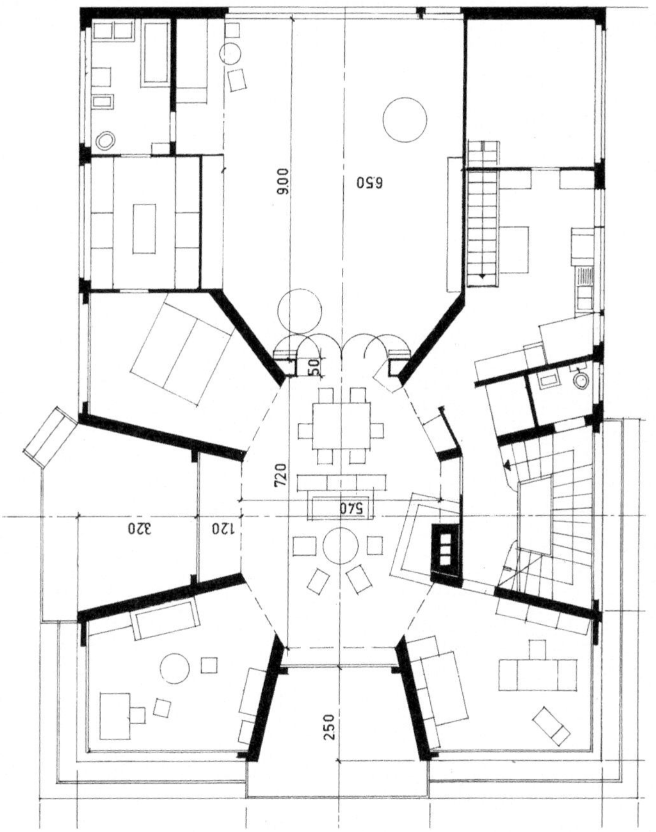

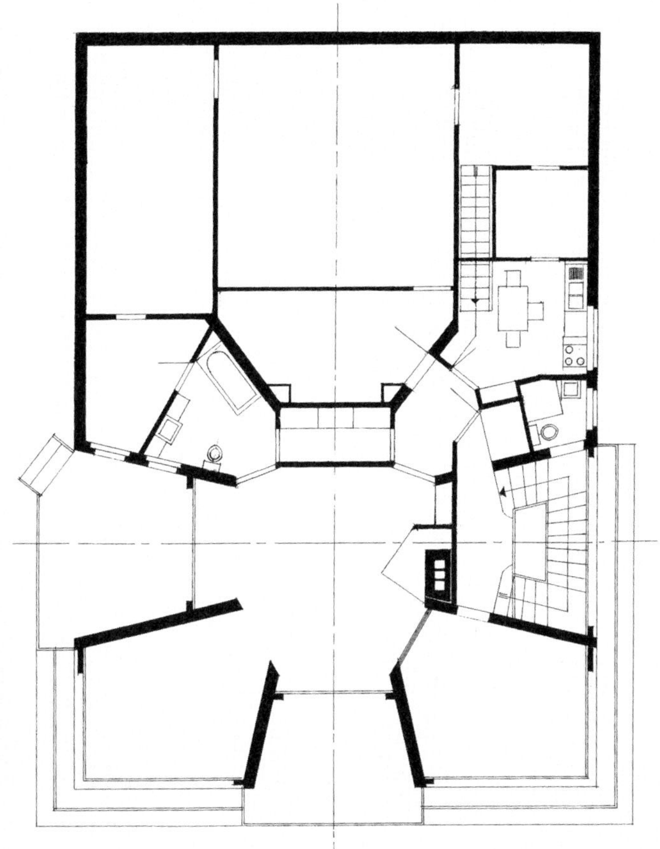

Plans No. 102–108

April 2, 1957

The ink drawings by Martin Steiger were created around ten months after the first sketch by Flora Steiger-Crawford. The studio is integrated into the rear facade. The kitchen in the lower apartment is now also on the east side, below that of the upper apartment. An in-line staircase connects the upper apartment with the lower shared laundry room.

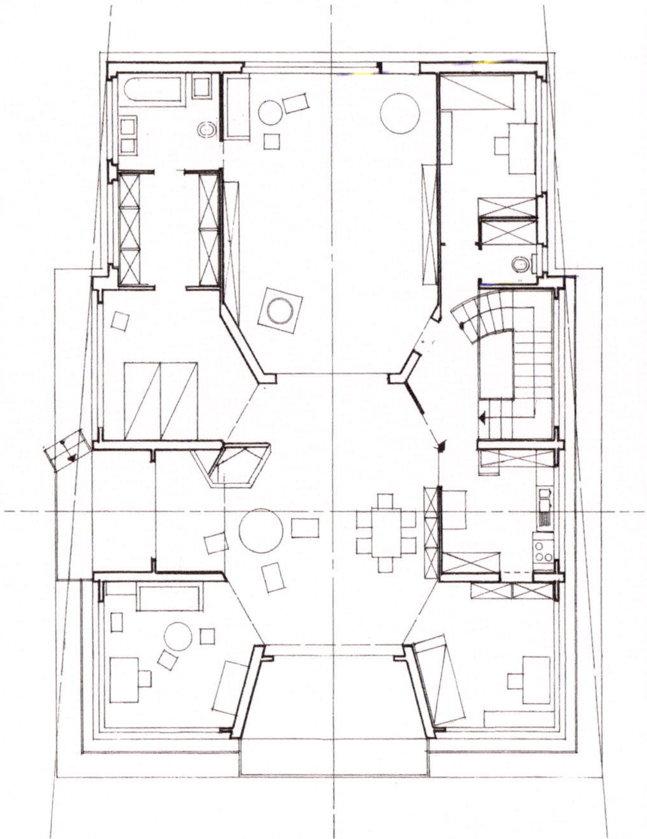

Plans No. 109–112

April 15, 1957

The radiating walls to the east and west are “rectified,” the staircase is displaced to the rear, the kitchens are moved to the front and connected to the central room. The fireplaces have been moved to the opposite west side. The circumferential cantilever slabs (balconies) are extended to the rear over the staircase, while the rear part is set back, thus giving a square format to the central floor plan.

The slabs in the vestibule are detached from the rear wall of the main building mass, forming a small console.

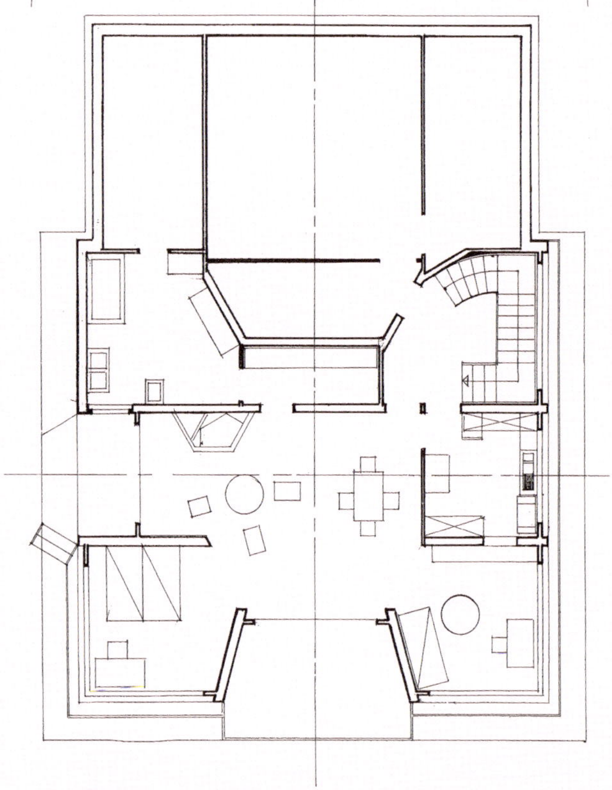

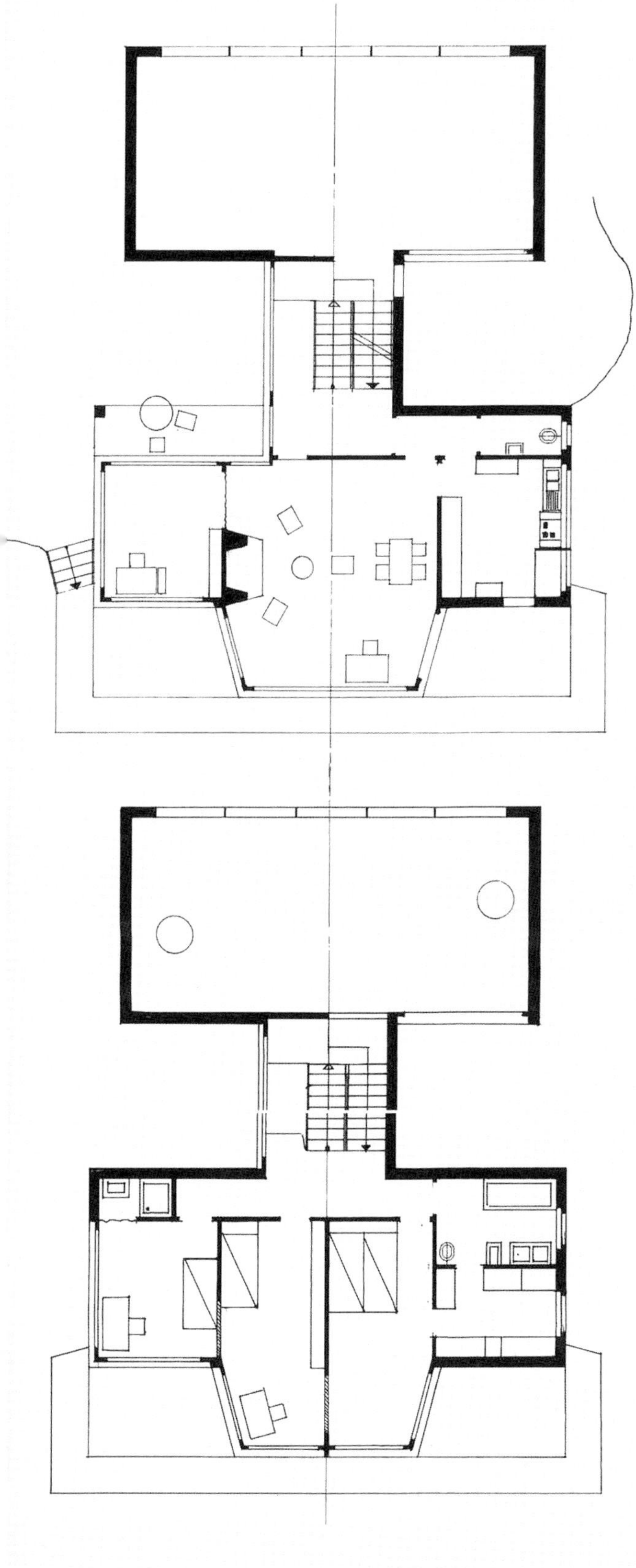

1:200

Plans No. 113–114

May 3, 1957

A completely new approach emerges: split level, two built volumes parallel to the slope with a staircase between, only one apartment: "living" at the bottom, the studio at the back in the middle, "sleeping" at the top. Not pursued further.

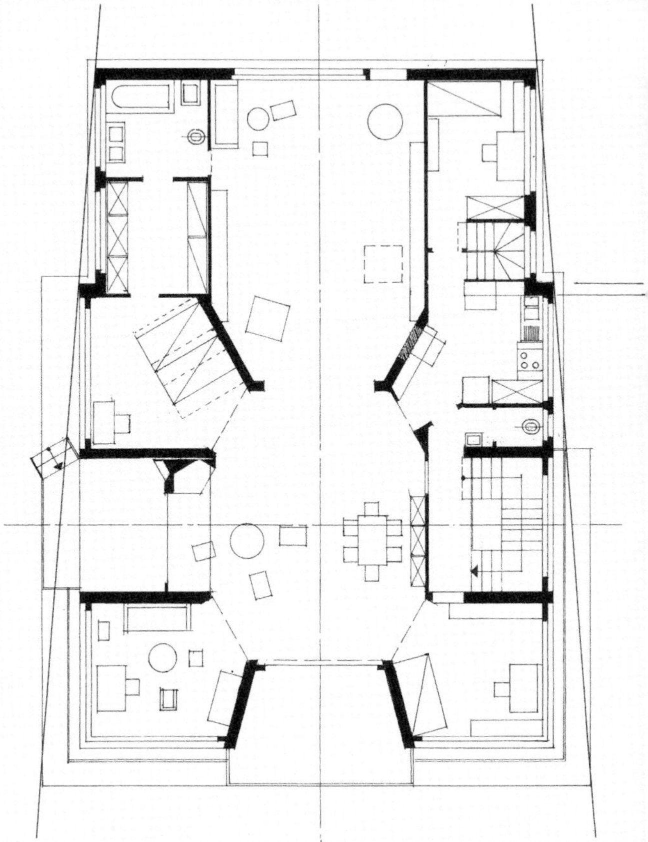

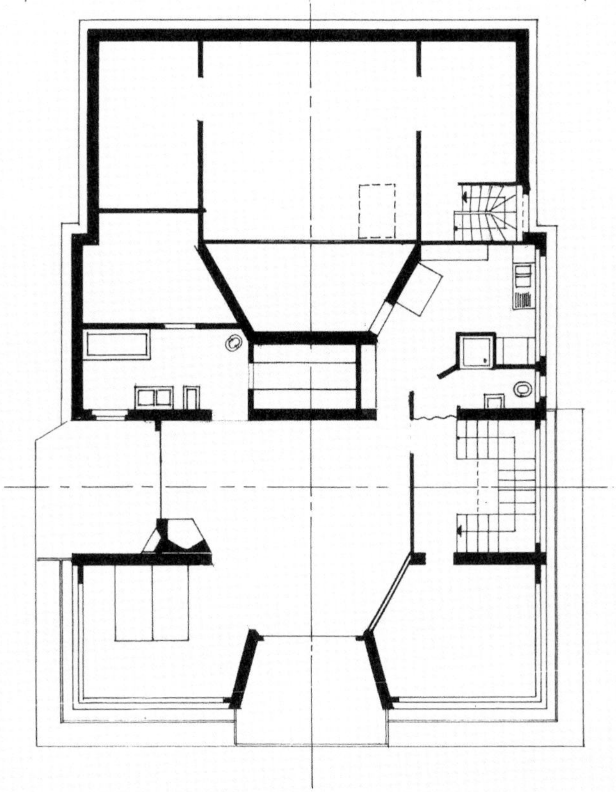

Plans No. 115–124

May 6, 1957

The next project variant returns to the previous arrangement of the staircase and kitchen, with the balcony moved back. Pragmatically, the kitchen and toilet mirror the shape of the bedroom on the opposite side. Corner projections at the rear still define the square, while the fireplace in the west loggia is moved to the south side of the lower apartment.

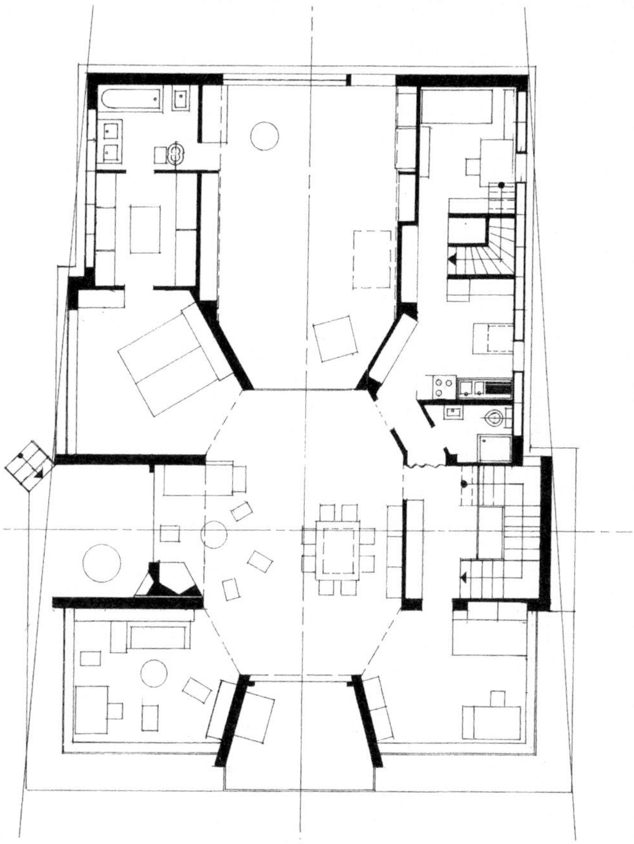

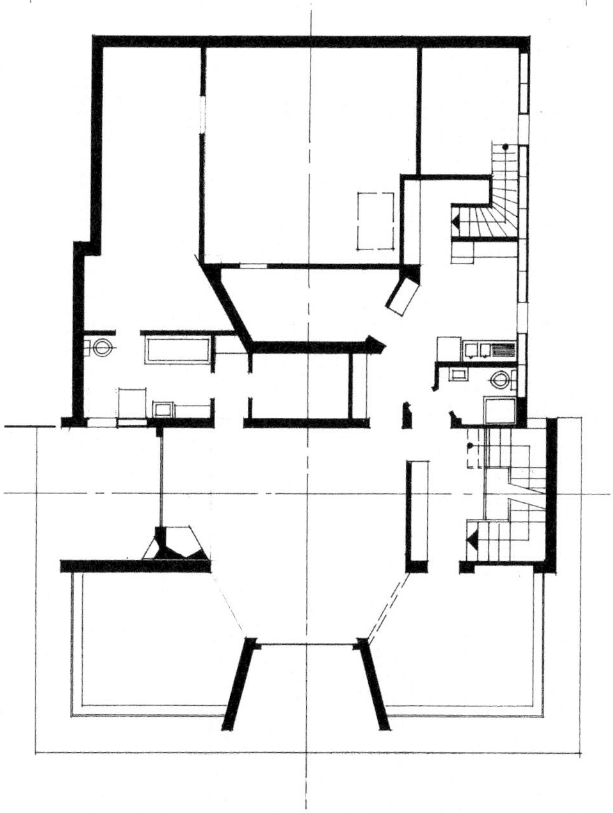

1:200

Plans No. 125–128

May 20, 1957

The front of the utility section (wash room, kitchen, servants' room) is straightened in the portion up to the staircase, ensuring that the stairwell is naturally lit, and the circumferential balcony running around the wall slab of the staircase is omitted. That means the square arrangement is abandoned, reinforcing the asymmetry of the floor plan.

The side facade with high-set ribbon windows and French windows corresponds to the version ultimately implemented.

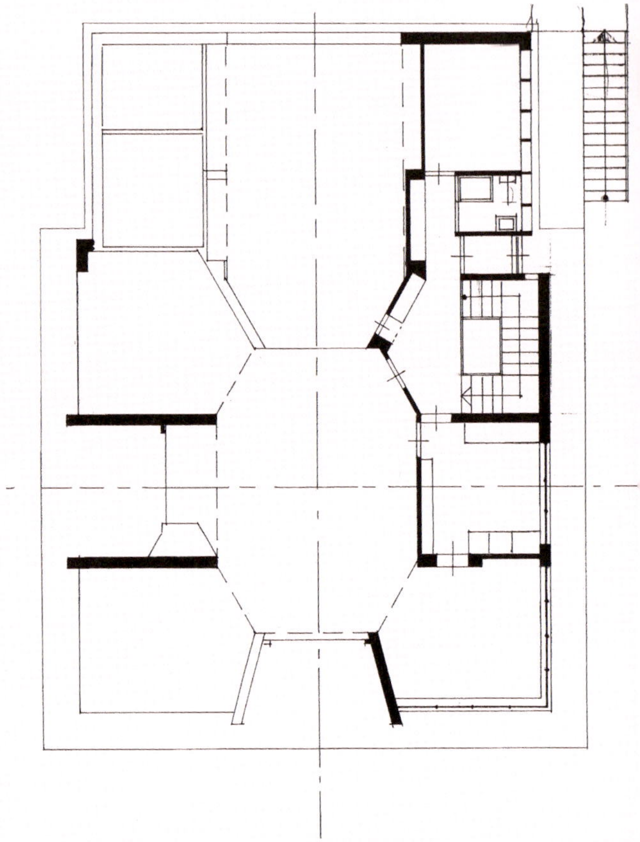

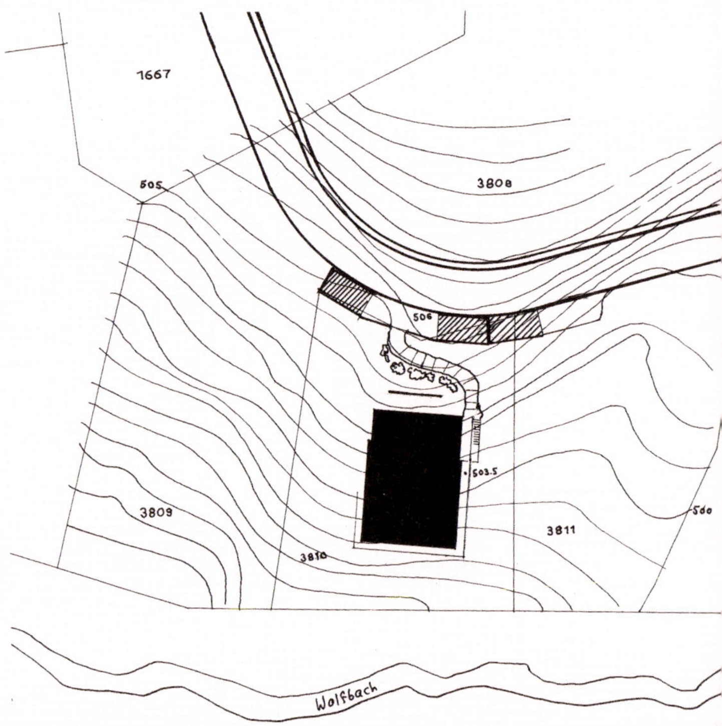

Plans No. 143–145

October 11, 1957

Five months later, another new approach is adopted. The house is accessed from above, from Belsitostrasse, and access on the valley side is no longer included. The house is now placed directly on the valley, a completely new situation. The position of the stairs and kitchen is “swapped” around again. Not pursued further.

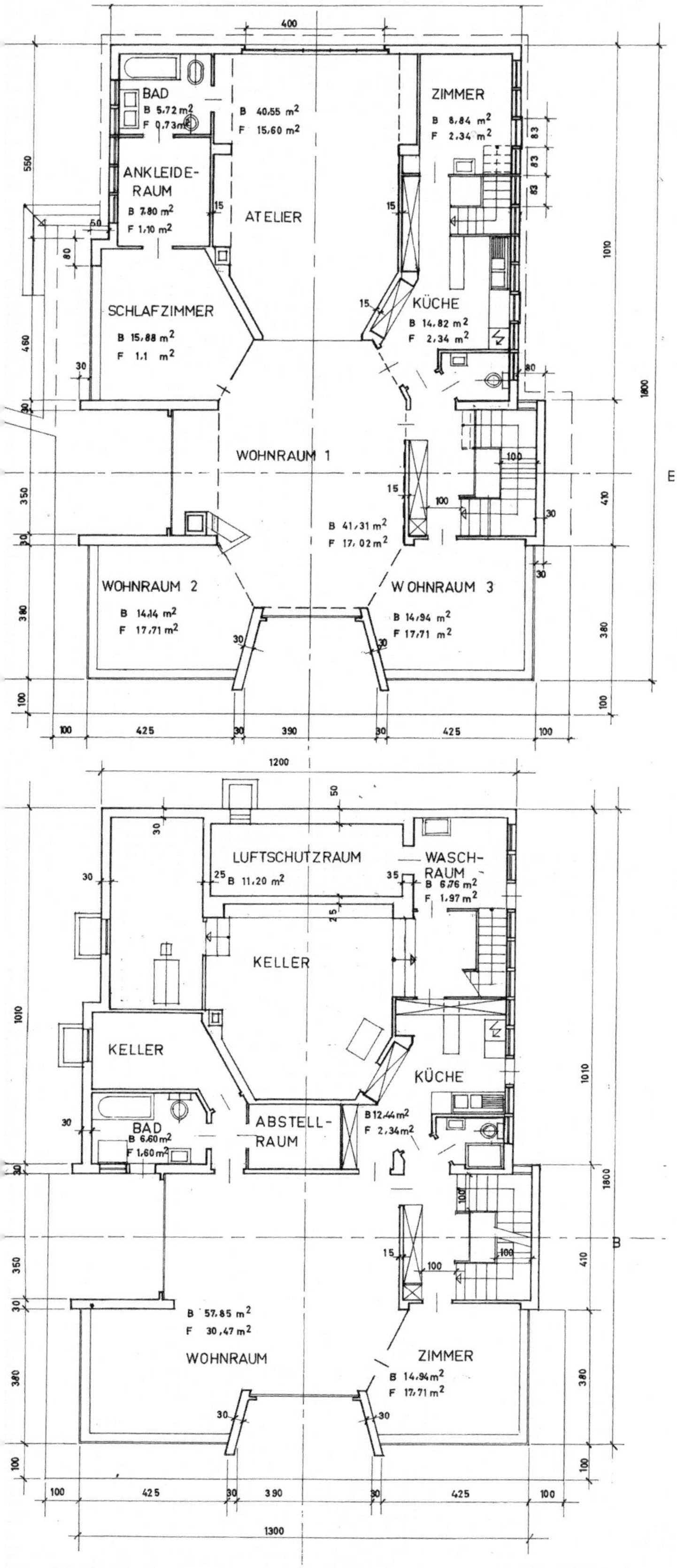

1:200

Plans No. 156–157

May 14, 1958

Application for planning permission, also for the extension. (Extension not realized until 1970.)

Resumption of the original project after an interruption of more than six months. The small restroom is still accessed from the staircase, the kitchen is parallel to the facade, the fireplace has been turned towards the central room, and the dimensions of the lower south-facing loggia have been slightly reduced.

Terracing of the site, outdoor space for the lower apartment, accessed via the kitchen. The supporting slabs for the entrance are replaced by free-standing pillars.

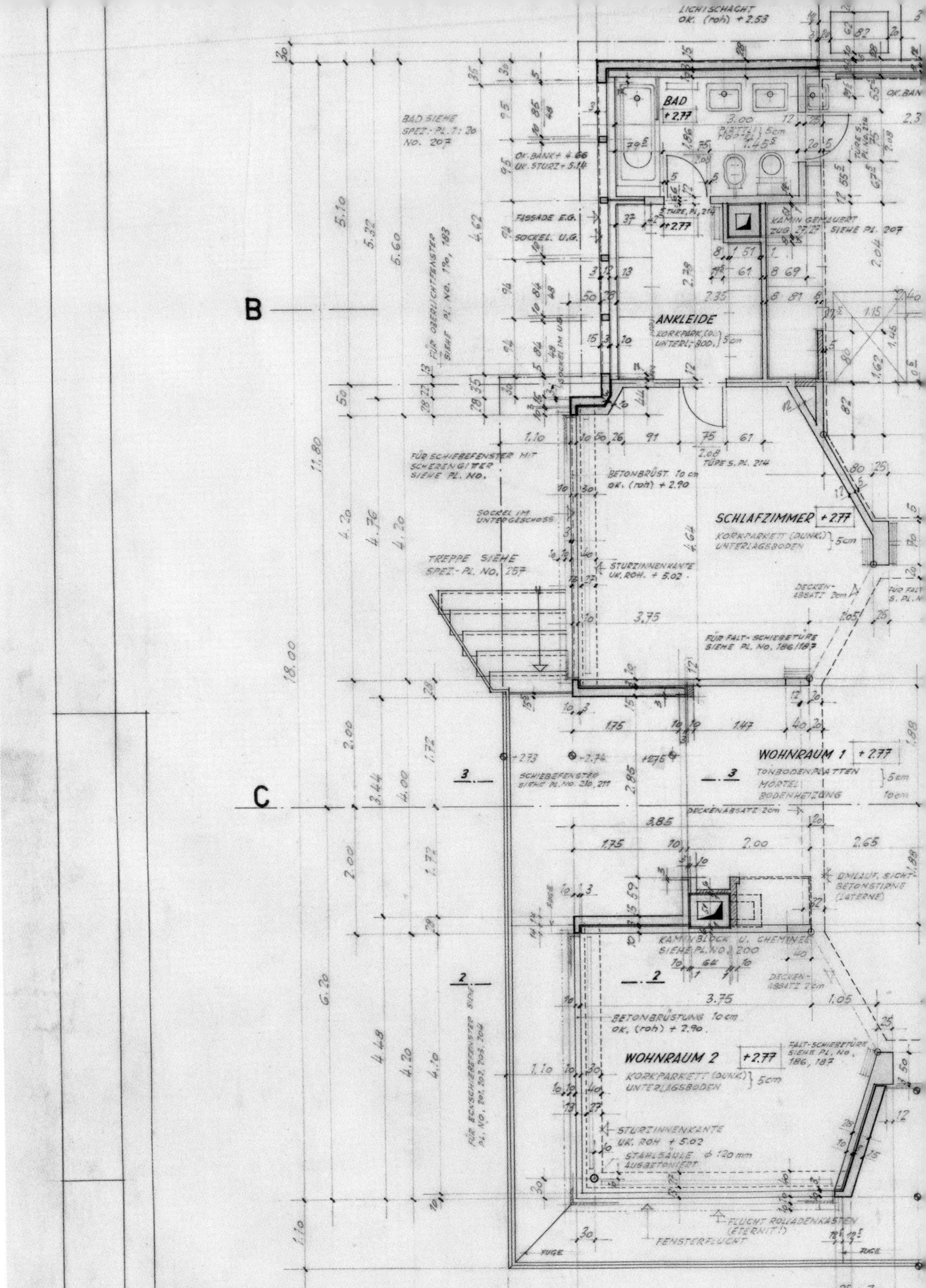

FÜR SCHNITT A-A : SIEHE PL. NO. 250
FÜR SCHNITT B-B : SIEHE PL. NO. 252
FÜR SCHNITT C-C : SIEHE PL. NO. 251

FÜR AUSSPARUNGEN (HEIZUNG, SANITÄR etc.) SIEHE SPEZ. AUSSPARUNGSPLAN!

±0 = 501.10 = O.K. FERTIGER FUSSBODEN UNTERGESCHOSS!

LEGENDE.

- EISENBETON
- ISOLIERSTEINMAUERWERK (MÖRTELMISCH. NACH. ANGABE D. BAULEITG.)
- ZELLTONPLATTEN - MAUERWERK
- KAMINMAUERWERK
- WÄRME - ISOLATION : KORK, SAGEX
- GRANIT
- SPÄTER AUFMAUERN
- MÖRTEL, RABITZ etc.
- HOLZ
- SANITÄRE APPARATE
- HEIZKÖRPER

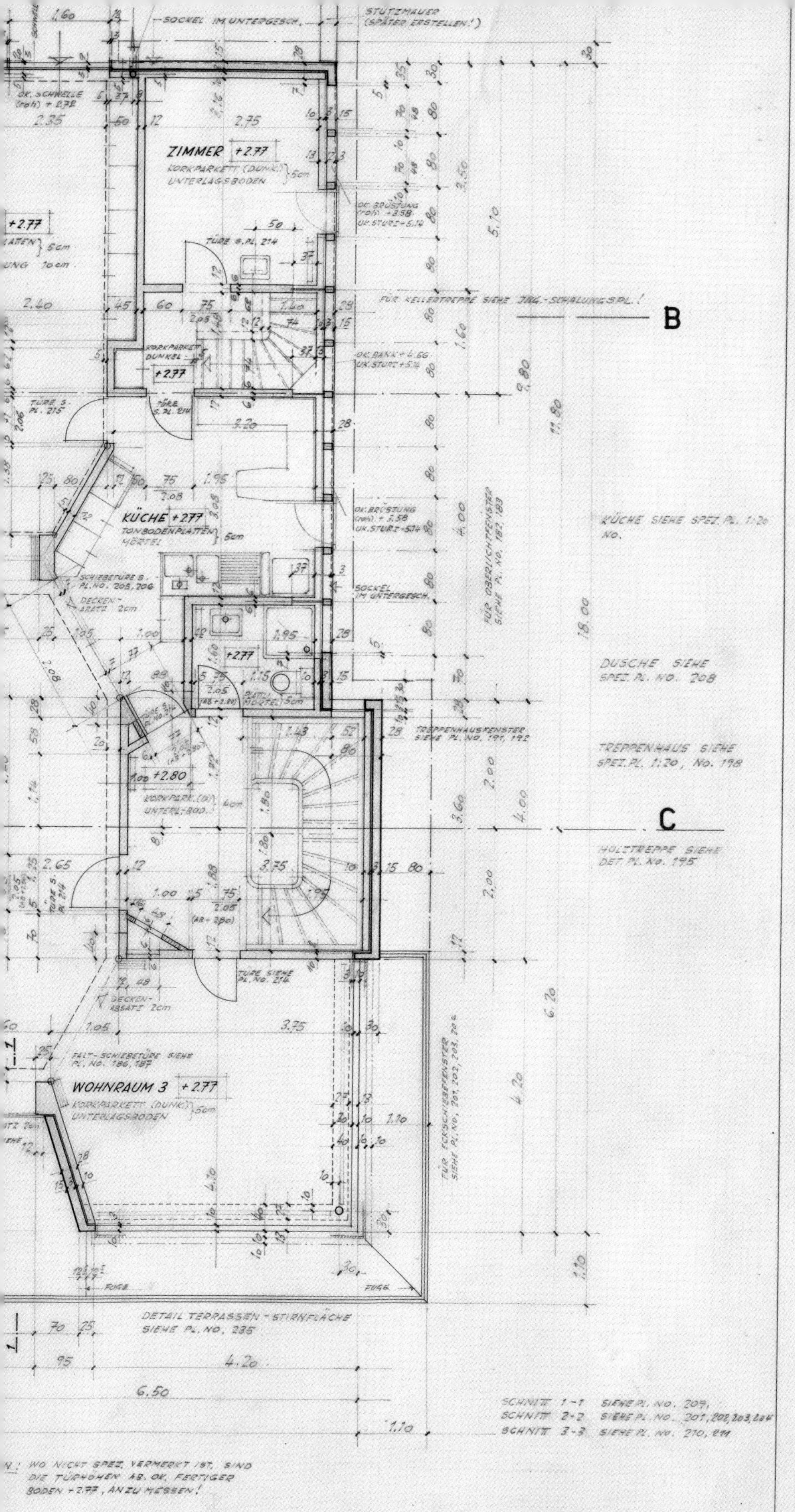
SOCKEL IM UNTERGESCH.
STÜTZMAUER (SPÄTER ERSTELLEN!)
OK. SCHWELLE (roh) + 2.72
ZIMMER +2.77
KORKPARKETT (DUNK.) UNTERLAGSBODEN 5cm
OK. BRÜSTUNG (roh) + 3.58 UK. STURZ + 5.14
TÜRE S. PL. 214
FÜR KELLERTREPPE SIEHE ING.-SCHALUNGS.PL.!
B
KORKPARKETT DUNKEL +2.77
OK. BANK + 4.66 UK. STURZ + 5.14
TÜRE S. PL. 215
TÜRE S. PL. 214
KÜCHE +2.77
TONBODENPLATTEN MÖRTEL 5cm
OK. BRÜSTUNG (roh) + 3.58 UK. STURZ + 5.14
FÜR OBERLICHTFENSTER SIEHE PL. NO. 182, 183
KÜCHE SIEHE SPEZ. PL. 1:20 NO.
SCHIEBETÜRE S. PL. NO. 205, 206
DECKENABSATZ 2cm
SOCKEL IM UNTERGESCH.
+2.77
PLATTEN MÖRTEL 5cm
DUSCHE SIEHE SPEZ. PL. NO. 208
TREPPENHAUSFENSTER SIEHE PL. NO. 191, 192
TREPPENHAUS SIEHE SPEZ. PL. 1:20, No. 198
+2.80
KORKPARK. (D) UNTERL.-BOD. 4cm
C
HOLZTREPPE SIEHE DET. PL. No. 195
TÜRE S. PL. 214
TÜRE SIEHE PL. NO. 214
DECKENABSATZ 2cm
FALT-SCHIEBETÜRE SIEHE PL. NO. 186, 187
WOHNRAUM 3 + 2.77
KORKPARKETT (DUNK.) UNTERLAGSBODEN 5cm
FÜR ECKSCHIEBEFENSTER SIEHE PL. NO. 201, 202, 203, 204
FUGE
FUGE
DETAIL TERRASSEN-STIRNFLÄCHE SIEHE PL. NO. 235
SCHNITT 1-1 SIEHE PL. NO. 209,
SCHNITT 2-2 SIEHE PL. NO. 201, 202, 203, 204
SCHNITT 3-3 SIEHE PL. NO. 210, 211
N.! WO NICHT SPEZ. VERMERKT IST, SIND DIE TÜRHÖHEN AB. OK. FERTIGER BODEN + 2.77, ANZUMESSEN!

ansicht von Osten   Horizont 497 m ü M

№ 151 b_2 26.10.57 ms

View from the east (Martin Steiger): V-shaped configuration, extension of the staircase slab in the form of a console-style projection as a load-bearing element for the ceiling. Three garages built into the slope.

Plans No. 29–35

June 20 / 26, 1956

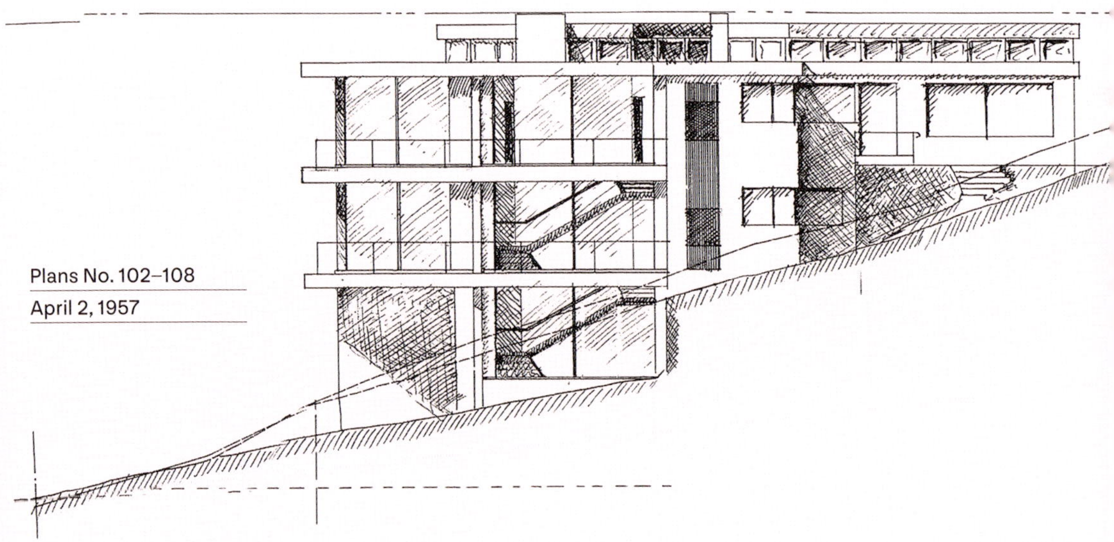

Plans No. 102–108

April 2, 1957

1:200

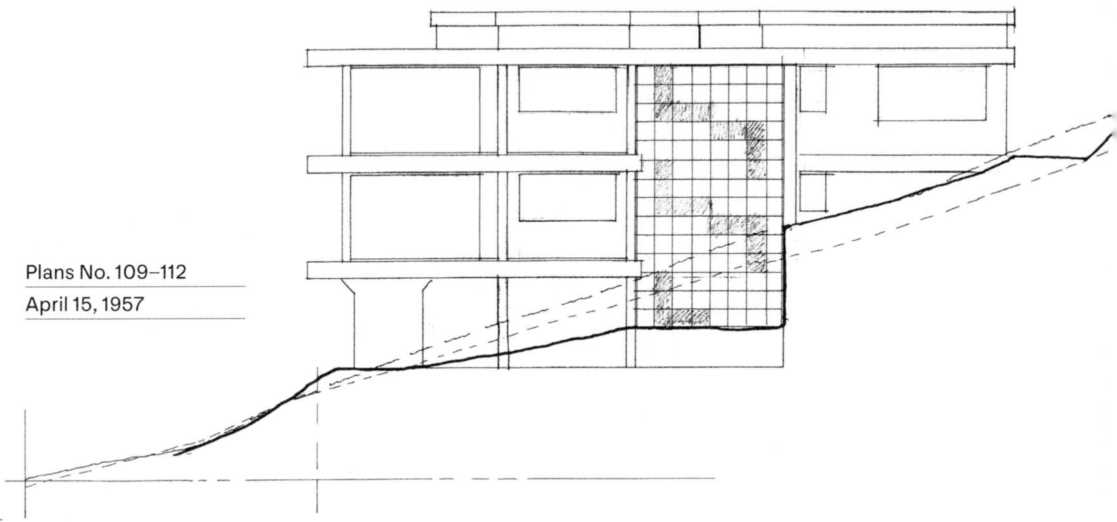

Plans No. 109–112

April 15, 1957

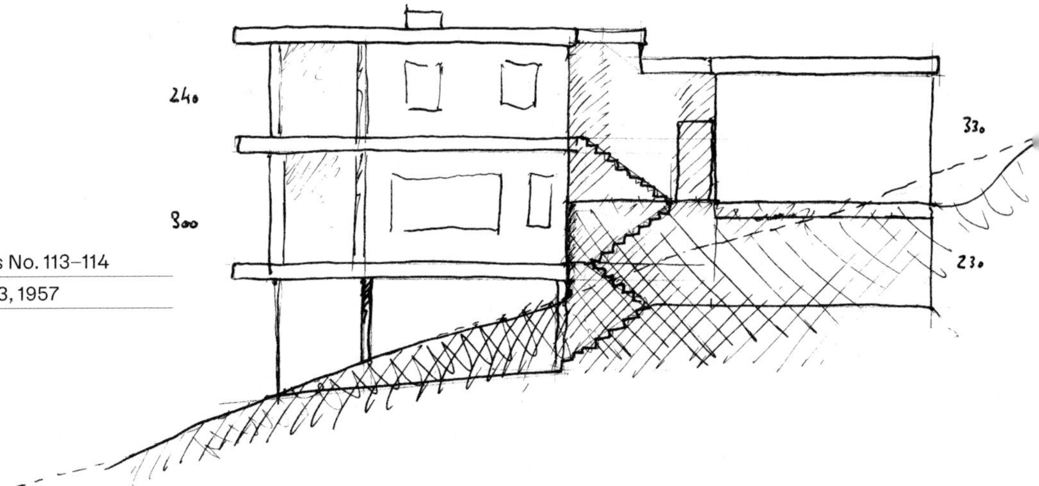

Plans No. 113–114

May 3, 1957

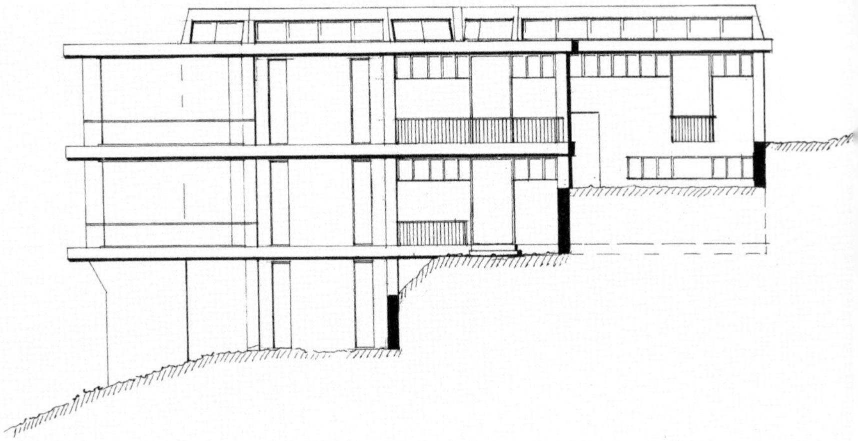

Plans No. 115–124

May 6, 1957

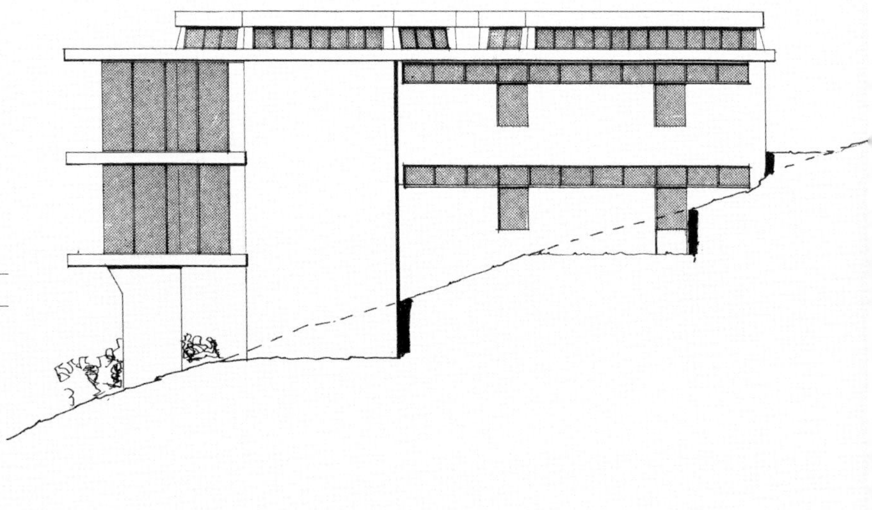

Plans No. 125–128

May 20, 1957

1:200

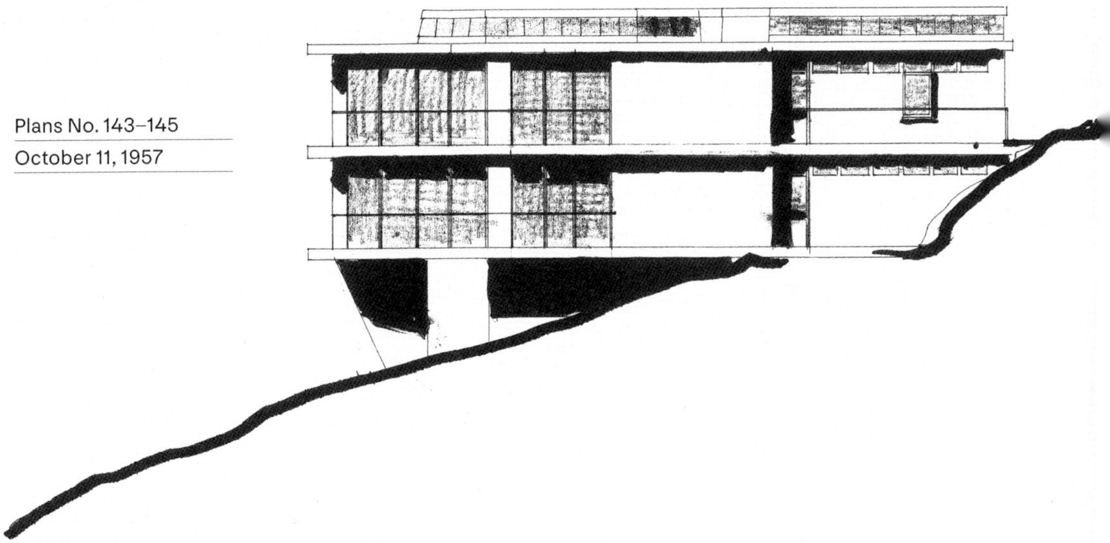

Plans No. 143–145
October 11, 1957

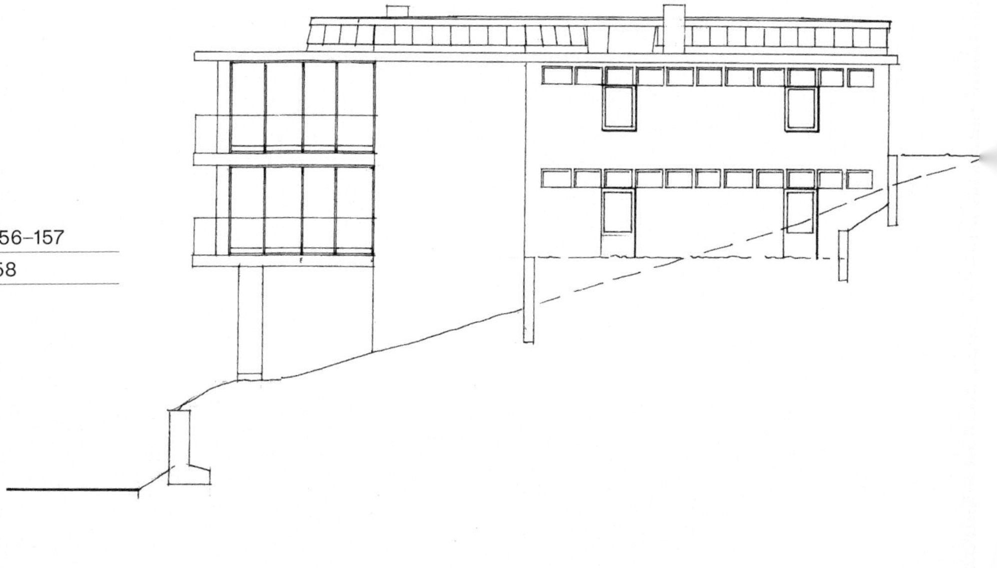

Plans No. 156–157
May 14, 1958

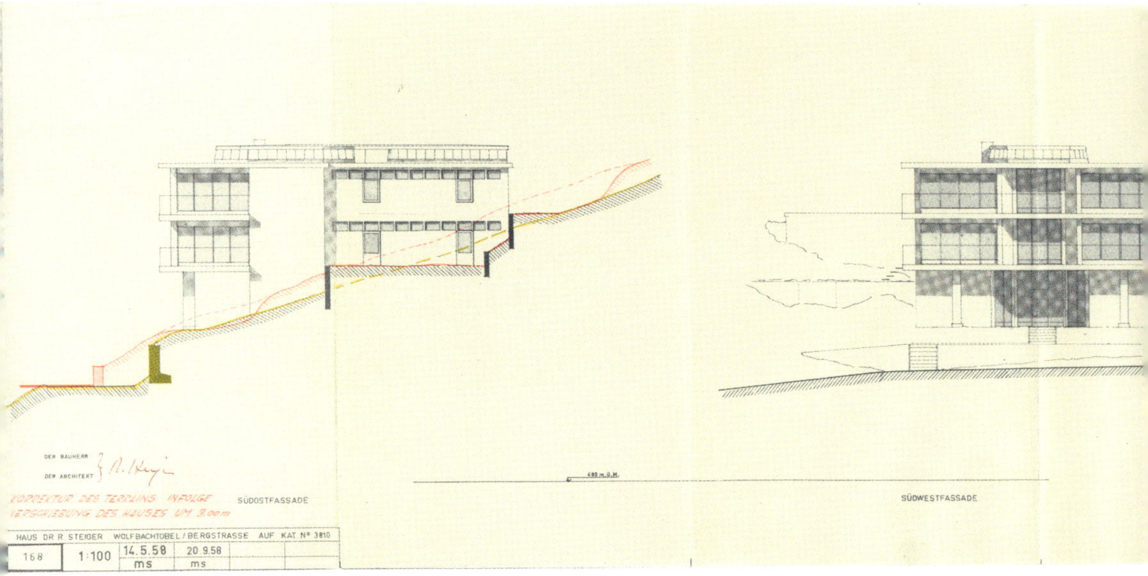

In the project as implemented, the house or rather the building line is set back three meters from the road, pushing the architecture more into the slope (see addendum to the application for planning permission dated December 19, 1958). This ensures the monumental entrance hall is sufficiently distant from the roadway and improves its spatial mise-en-scène. The two entrance hall pillars with their highly sculptural design become the hallmark of the building in the ravine.

1:400

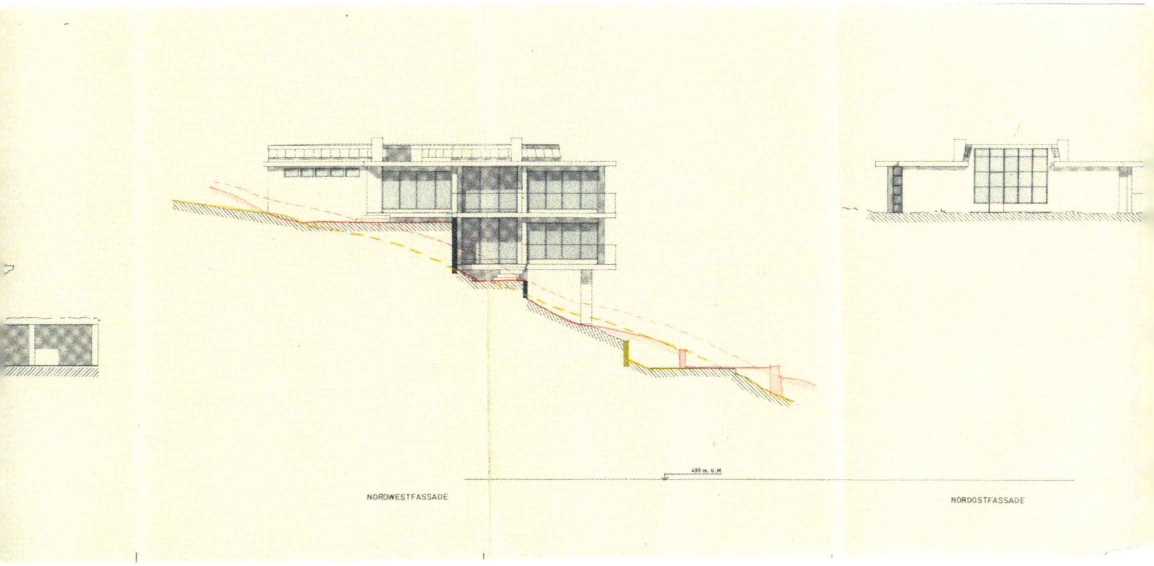

Typology

Spatial Relations

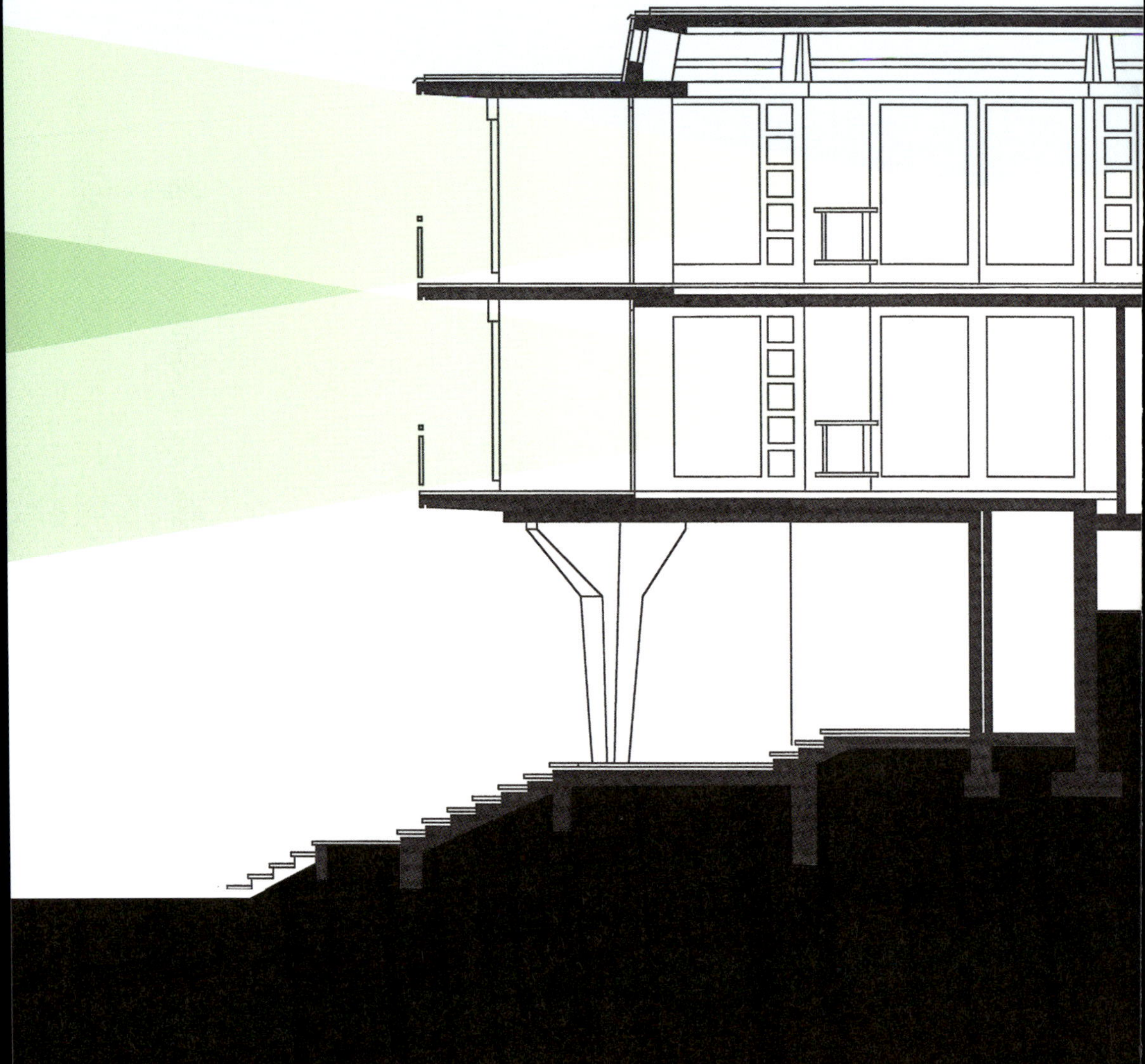

The sloping site and thus the section becomes the element that generates the design. A monumental entrance hall, highlighted by two sculptural pillars, is set in front of the plinth wall, which is continued on the west side as a retaining wall for the garden.

The spatial focus looking out of the upper apartment is in particular northward, toward the slope, while the lower apartment offers a “compressed” panoramic vista to the south. Setting the skylights in the upper apartment above the central space, on the other hand, underscores its centrality.

As visitors enter, they first encounter the concave indentation in the plinth and are guided and directed to the staircase at the side. Moving in the opposite direction, when leaving the house, the path ends abruptly “almost in the forest,” as Dieter Kienast writes.

Angle of Vision

"Open"

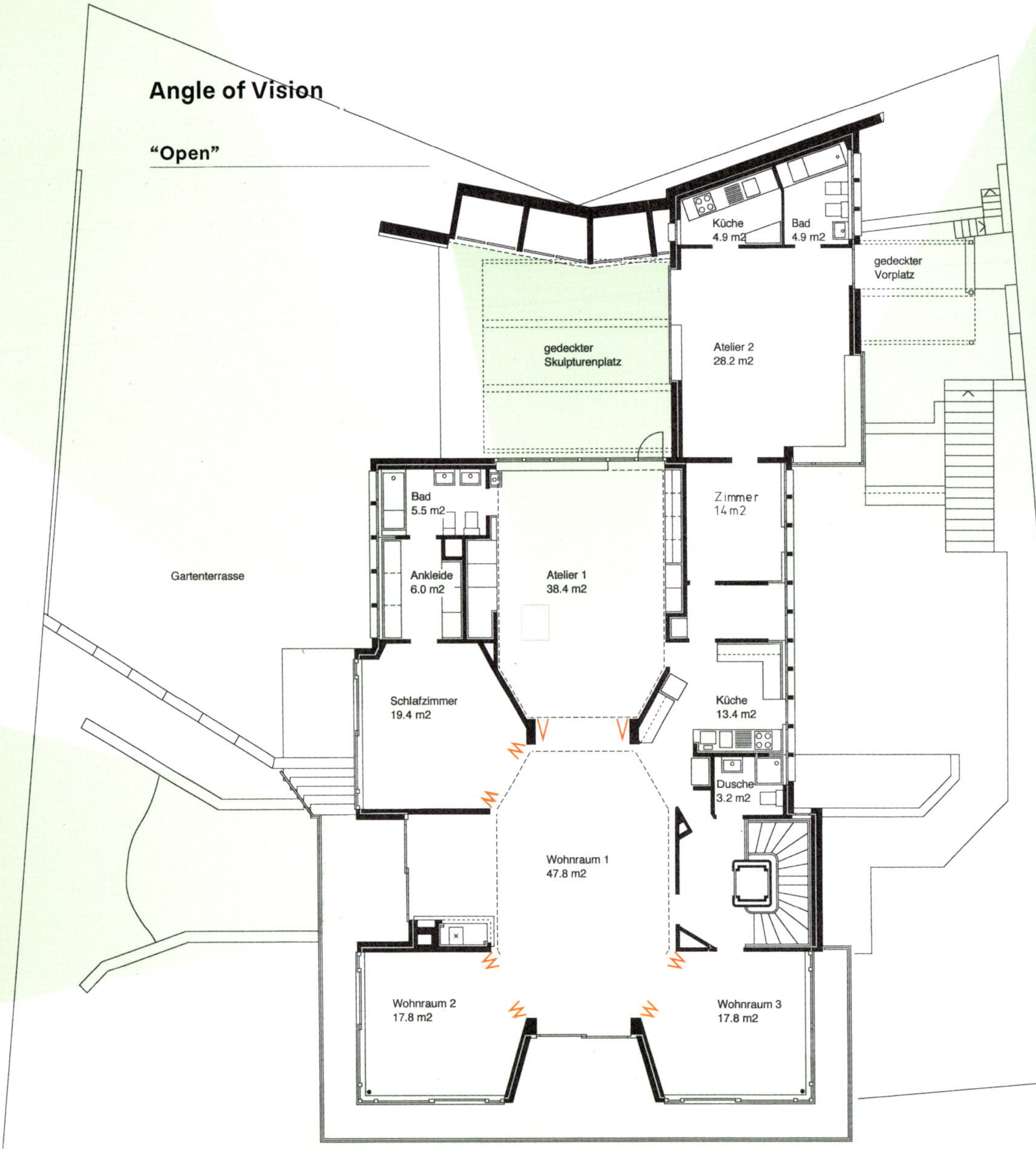

The Upper Apartment

The three corner rooms, accessed via folding doors, are docked onto the hallway. The striking, small-format windows underscore the corners of the rooms and frame the internal steel support. The fourth corner room on the east side is "missing." It has been replaced by a functional, linear unit that extends into the depth of the building as a utility section with bathroom, kitchen and ancillary rooms. The studio at the rear, on the north side, anchors the building towards the slope. As a result, the house is not only oriented towards the south, but also, with the door to the studio open, towards the north on the slope-facing side.

"Closed"

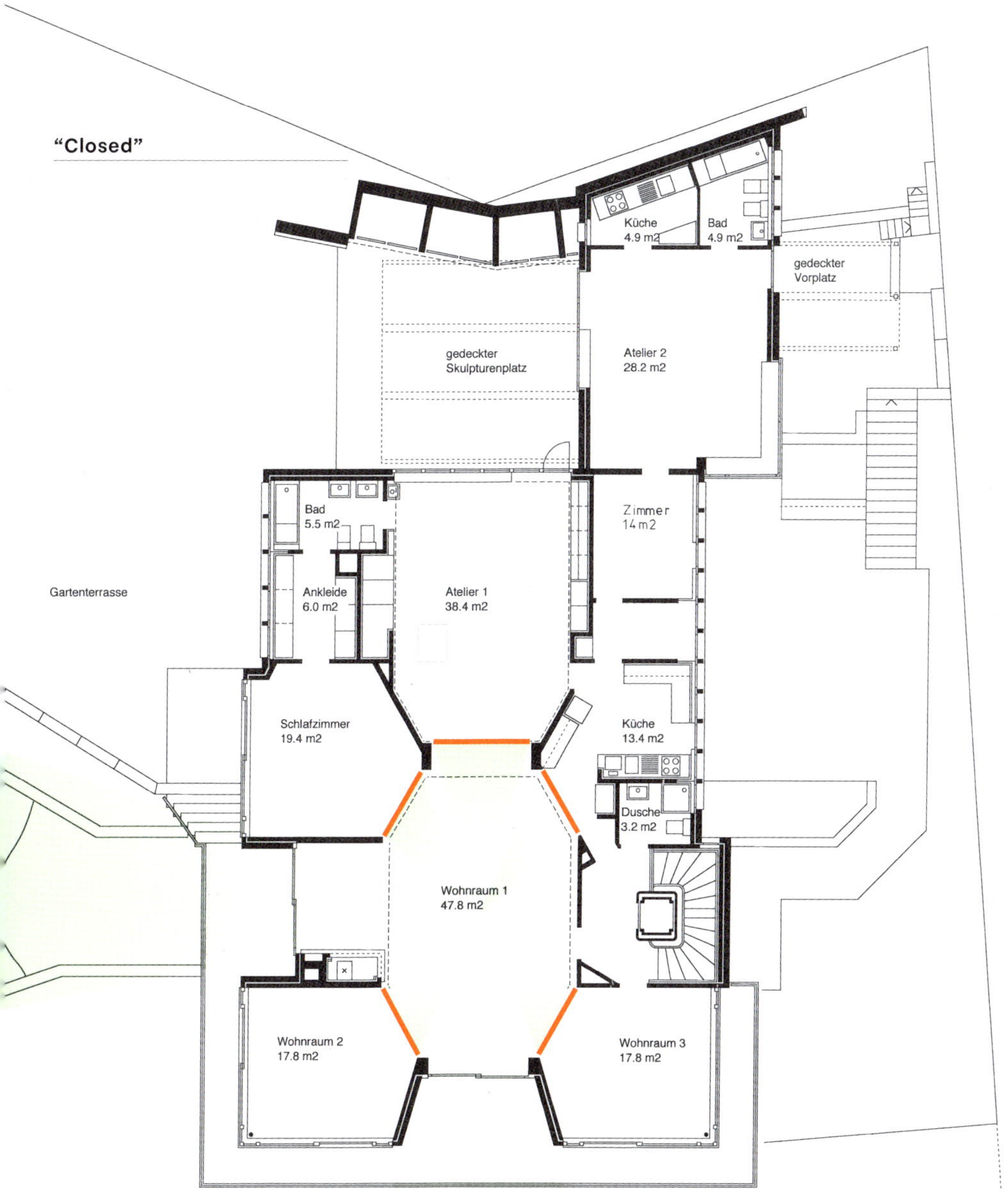

1:200

On both floors, two entrances lead into each of the two apartments. The middle entrance leads directly into the central room, a kind of living room-cum-hallway.[15] There is no cloakroom. The side entrance leads into the kitchen and, after turning through 180 degrees, into the central space too. There are also two further entrances, into the southern corner room and to an additional restroom in the stairwell. A central space is created when the doors are closed.

The plans show the building in its current configuration after the 1991 refurbishment with the extension from 1970.

15 — On the subject of the hallway, see inter alia, Katharina Stehrenberger, "Die Diele. Tanzboden der Architektur," in *Werk, Bauen + Wohnen* 7/8, 2021, pp. 6–13.

"Open"

When the folding doors are open, a radial, permeable space is created in the spirit of Flora Steiger-Crawford's sketch (1956). The interior spaces are connected with the green of the exterior by means of cross-references that run diagonally (hall – corner room – forest), as well as axially (hall – fireplace – garden room) as sequence of spaces.

The Lower Apartment

The lower apartment adopts the upper apartment's structure as a footprint, while incorporating pragmatic adaptations. Due to the sloping site, the rear corner room on the east side is omitted. The rear wall of the cellar is raised up to this floor. It provides stability for the apartment. Two doors lead to the rear area with the "service" rooms. Below the studio is a sculpture cellar, connected by an aperture in the ceiling. The spatial effect is more subdued – there are no skylights, in contrast to the upper apartment – and the interior-exterior relationship is mainly east-west, parallel to the gorge.

“Closed”

When the folding doors are closed, a central room is created with the gaze directed toward the exterior, immediately onto/across the garden room to the west, “opening up” to the south towards the edge of the forest.

The spatial relationships, which can be altered by means of the folding doors shown in the photos by Leonardo Finotti, make the Steiger House so compelling.

Excursion

Gio Ponti (1891–1979) – Visual References

In the early 1960s, Gio Ponti developed a new design instrument for examining spatial relationships, taking the phrase *joie d'y vivre* (joy of living there) as his motto. Using perspectives from hand-picked vantage points, he studied a range of views and thus spatial constellations, often spanning several rooms.

(A)

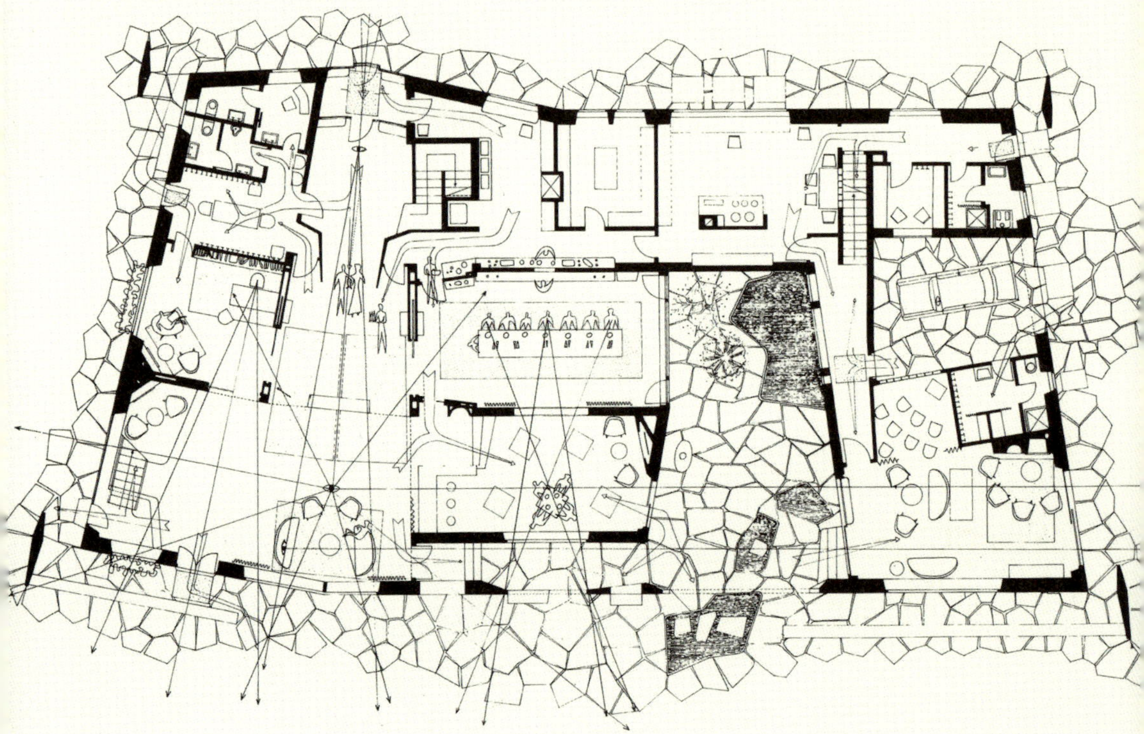

Comparable to the Steiger House is the Villa Nemazee (A) in Tehran (1960), in which the elongated entrance area functions as a prelude to the central hall with its various longitudinal and transverse views. An earlier project is the Villa Planchart (B) in Caracas (1967). On the first and upper story, Ponti illustrates how the views through the building and vistas looking out constantly change when moving through the building. The house becomes a kind of walk-in sculpture, in contrast to the Steiger House's more static, concentric conception.

1:400

(B)

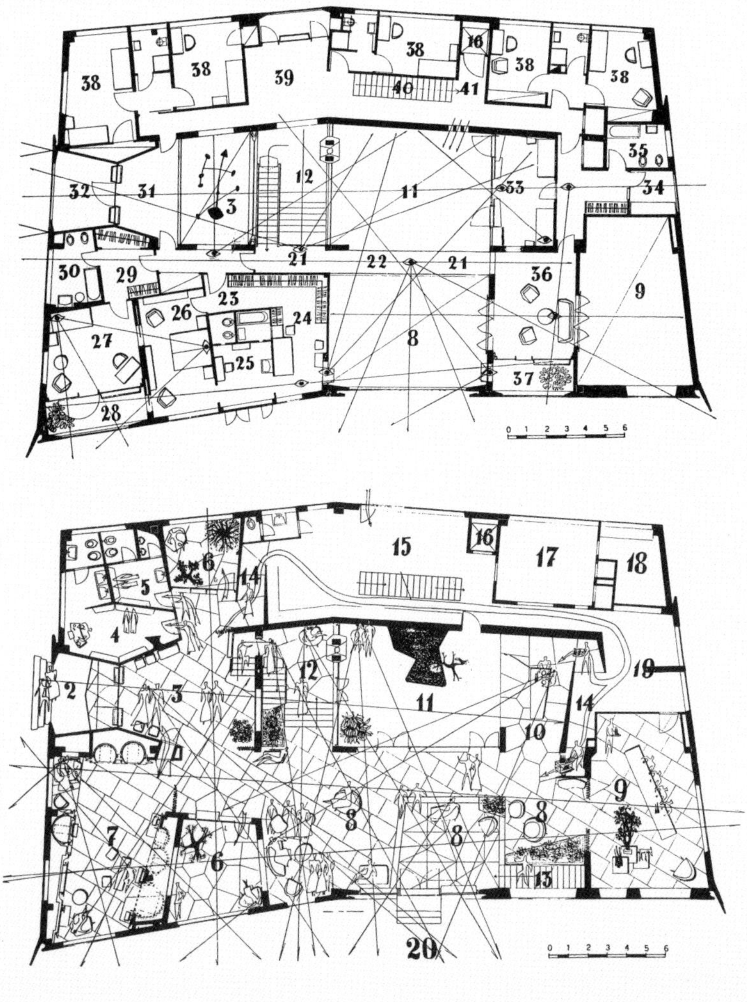

Vincenzo Scamozzi (1548–1616) – Rays of Light

In contrast to Palladio's Villa Rotonda (see page 80), whose schematic floor plan probably explains its positive reception, Villa Rocca by Vincenzo Scamozzi has a more balanced floor plan and section. As with the Rotonda, the dome is also 30 feet (1 piede vicentino 35.74 cm) in diameter.[16] Integrating both atria into the building means the modest access corridors found in the Rotonda are no longer required and instead become spacious loggias. Similarly to the interior of the Steiger House, rays of light influence the relationship between the loggias and the central hall, defined by the "delimitations" created by window and door reveals, building edges, and columns. In the windows of the corner rooms, for example, rays of light radiate from the outer edge of the window reveal to its opposite inner edge. The incident light sets up a distinction between illuminated and non-illuminated zones in the room, while also defining the distribution of shade on the inside of the outer walls (indirect light, direct light, diffuse light).

"Angle of visions," "visual references" and "light beams" are comparable concepts to some extent. They examine and give visual expression to the spatial relationship between adjacent rooms and sequences of spaces within them, considered on the one hand looking from the interior to the exterior (sight lines), and on the other hand looking in the opposite direction (incident light).

The lateral salons are open and offer a vista of the landscape. This results in generous views through the building and spatial interconnections to all four sides. The anterooms of the corner chambers and the two staircases are also directly connected to the central room via alcoves.

In the project as implemented [(D)], the four corner chambers are reduced to two. This straightens up the floor plan. The smaller rooms (ancillary rooms) are located to the rear with a single entrance from the hallway. The two stairwells have been rotated and are accessed via the niches with a small, two-story forecourt – an unexpectedly "modern" spatial configuration. The two large corner rooms on the entrance side are rotated by 90 degrees and are likewise accessed directly from the hall via the two alcoves.

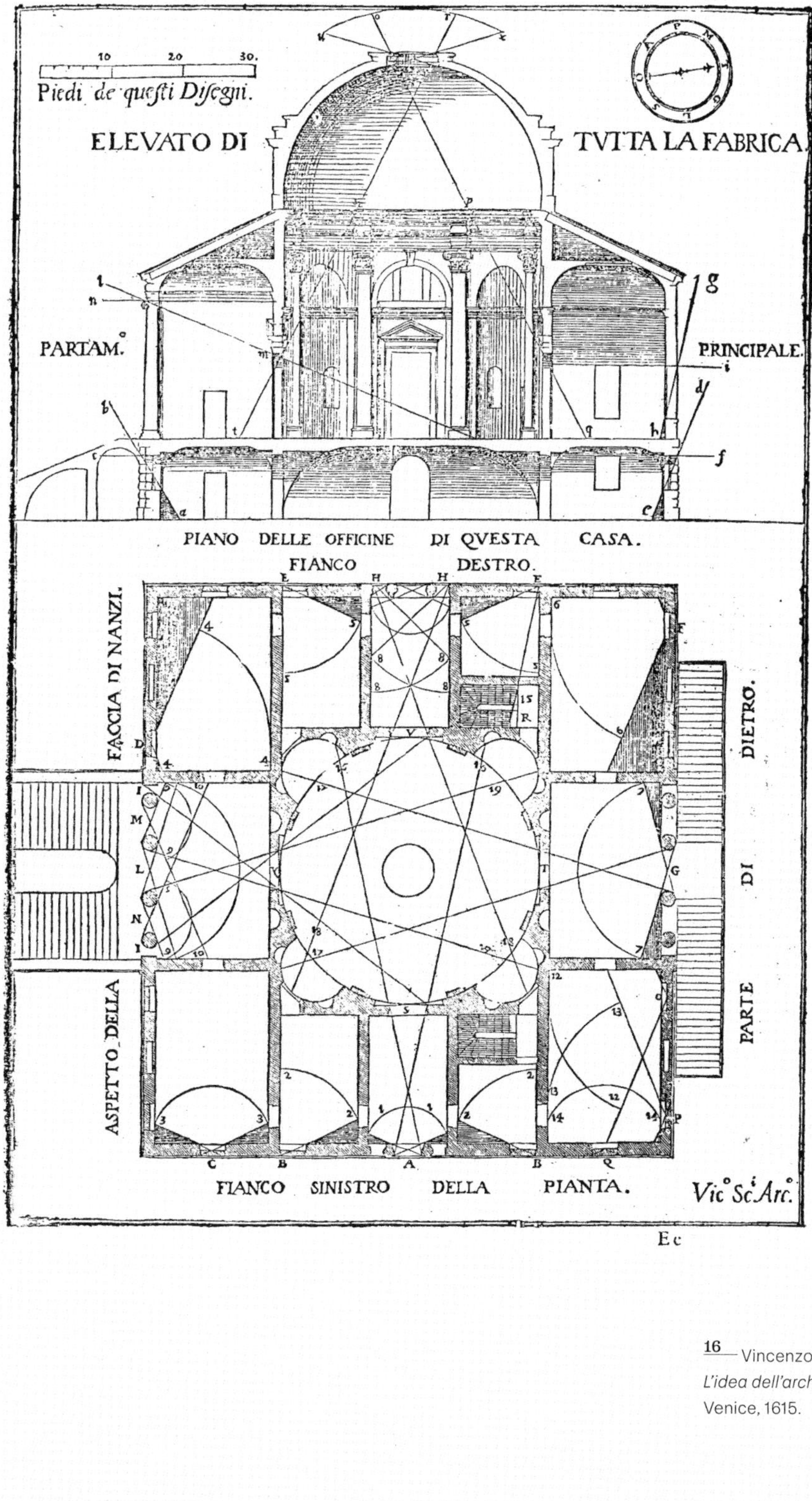

1:300

16 — Vincenzo Scamozzi, *L'idea dell'architettura universale*, Venice, 1615.

Andrea Palladio (1508–1580) – Central Floor Plan

The Steiger House makes a spectacular and unusual typological choice: a classical, horizontal central floor plan set on a slope. This becomes the project's "pièce de resistance" and thus the driving force in the design. It was a familiar theme for Flora Steiger-Crawford and Rudolf Steiger. As students, they visited Palladio's Villa La Rotonda (C) [17] with their professor Karl Moser. An early, circular project (1921) (A) from Rudolf Steiger's student days also references the central floor plan and recalls the country estate La Gordanne from 1810 on Lake Geneva.[18]

From the General to the Specific – An "Contaminated" Palladio

The conflict inherent in the contrast between building type (central space) and location (sloping site) forms the foundation underpinning the Steiger House and constitutes its essence, including the spatial and volumetric tension of the building volume. The two-story service section on the east side with its high-set ribbon windows is contrasted with the stepped west side. The difference between the two sides is indirectly a consequence of the undulating topography. This gives rise to a swirling form, a kind of vortex. The central floor plan is "deformed," becoming a specific solution, in complete contrast to Casa Tonini (1974) by Reichlin & Reinhart, for example, which "strives for the basic shape inherent in all of Palladio's villas."[19]

The Steiger House (B) is therefore a kind of "contaminated" Palladio. The montage (mirroring) hypothetically "completes" the floor plan to form a classical, Palladian typology.

(A)

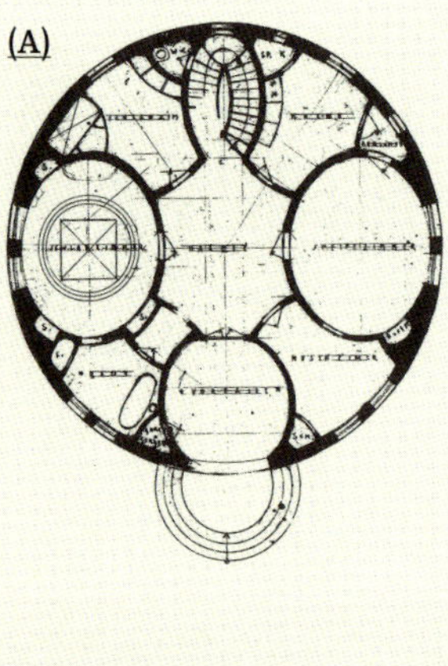

(B)

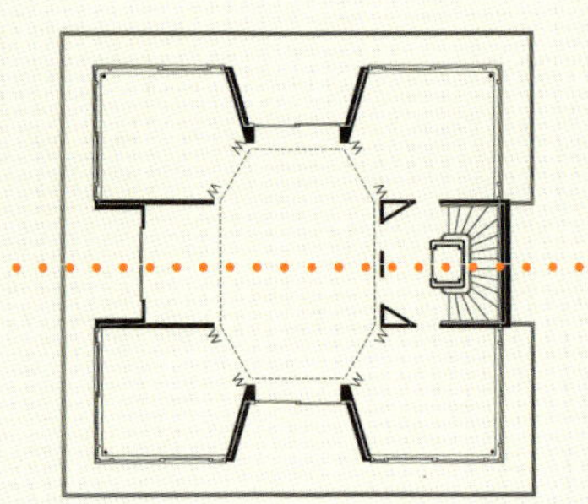

(C)

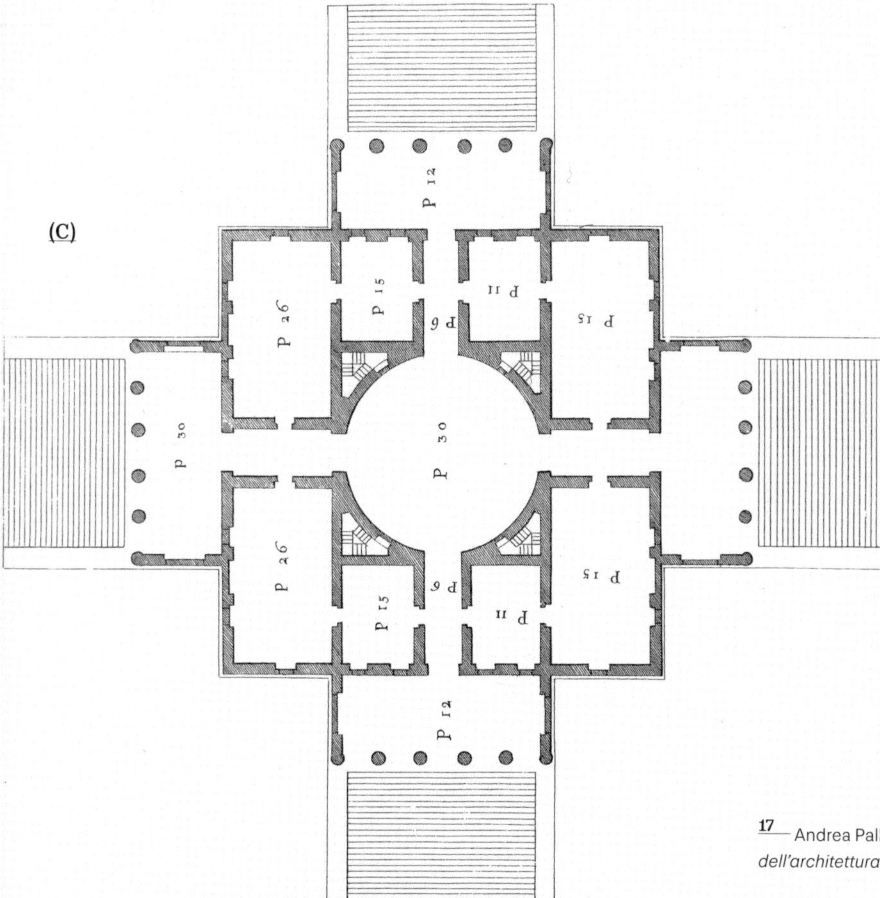

1:400

(D)

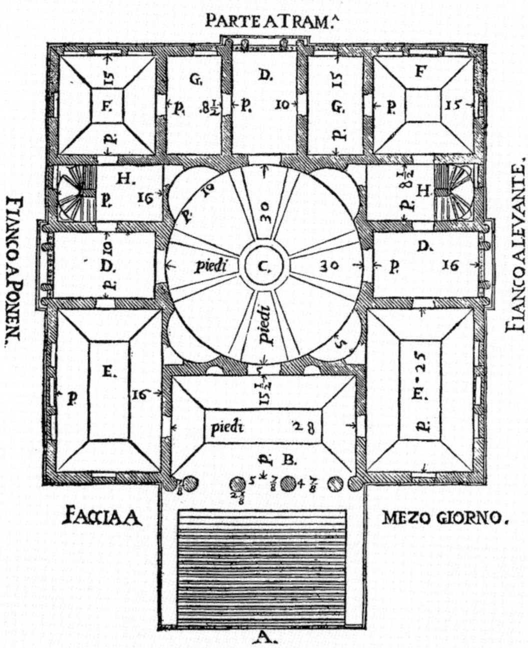

17 — Andrea Palladio, *I quattro libri dell'architettura*, Venice, 1570.

18 — Cf. *Die Präsenz Palladios in der Schweizer Architektur*, ed. ETH Zurich, exhib. cat., Kunstgewerbemuseum Zurich, Zurich, 1975, p. 10 f.

19 — In 1975, Paul Hofer and his colleagues presented a chronological series of ten buildings in Switzerland dedicated to Palladianism. Most are based on a central plan. The oldest example is the summer residence La Poya in Fribourg, completed in 1701, and the most recent is the Casa Tonini in Torricella by Bruno Reichlin and Fabio Reinhart from 1974. Hofer quotes the two architects as follows: "The scheme of the building in this case means the type as abstraction. It is not the ground plan of a specific villa that is being adopted here, but rather the basic form inherent in all of Palladio's villas, as revealed by Wittkower in his systematic study." ibid., p. 10 f.

Esch Sintzel Architects – "Buildings Live in the Present and Not in the Past" [20]

The concept of an apartment with no hallway, an important trend in residential construction in recent years, again updates the type of central space, as the following example by architects Esch Sintzel shows.

"The floor plan of the Crawford-Steiger House is almost Palladian in its structural clarity, even toughness, but at the same time it is soft and open in its changeability. This applies to the scope to shape the relationships that can exist between the spaces, as well as to the programmatic ascription of functions to the rooms. [...] We are currently trying to transfer the qualities of this role model from its upper-middle-class milieu to the modest circumstances found in standard rental housing." (Philipp Esch)[21]

Philipp Esch's explicit reference to the Steiger House testifies to the robustness of its typology and its potential. Mirroring the floor plan creates a two-unit house with apartments that display excellent spatial qualities and "spatial efficiency." In contrast to the Steiger House, the corner rooms are illuminated via the intermediate loggias, giving the central space a new, lateral orientation.

EMI Architekt*innen: Performative Living

EMI Architekt*innen go one step further with their performative residential building.[22] Revolving doors, movable furniture parts, and luminaires create ever-changing views through the building, along with perpetually new spatial constellations (day and night zones). In contrast to Le Corbusier's and Charlotte Perriand's scholarly studies on the *cellule de 14 m² par habitant* (14 m² module study per inhabitant)[23] the performative residential building is playful in nature. "Pleasurable like a Tinguely sculpture," Elli Mosayebi comments,[24] in opposition to the more modest "open/half-open/closed" interplay of the mobile folding doors in the Steiger House.

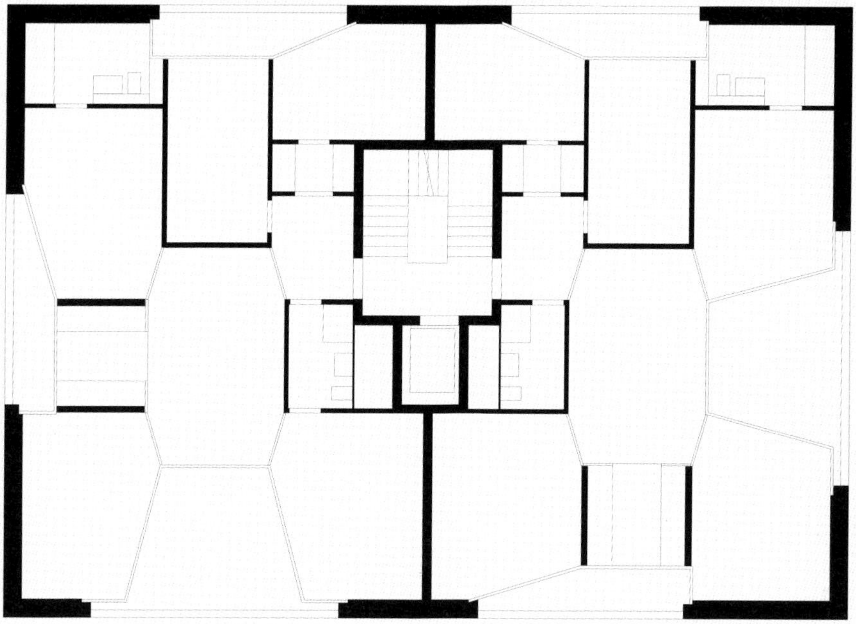

1:200

Esch Sintzel Architekten

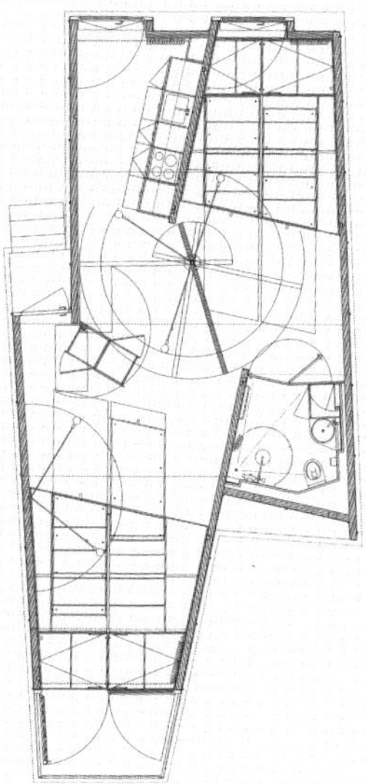

EMI Architekt*innen

20 — Yvonne Farrell, Shelley McNamara, in conversation with Christian Sumi and Marianne Burkhalter. Grafton Architects Dublin.

21 — Quote by Esch Sintzel.

22 — Cf. inter alia, Palle Petersen, "Der bewegte Plan," in *Hochparterre* 9/19, pp. 30–37.

23 — Cf. Christian Sumi, *Immeuble Clarté Genf 1932. Von Le Corbusier & Pierre Jeanneret*, Zurich, gta/Ammann, 1989, p. 112–113.

24 — See, Palle Petersen, op. cit., pp. 30–37.

Peter Steiger (1928–2023) – An Early Building

The hexagonal hall with the surrounding skylights and sliding doors in the extension to an existing facility in Boldern,[25] built in 1948 by Rudolf Steiger and Bruno Giacometti, is reminiscent of the Steiger House's octagonal central hall. Peter Steiger commented in conversation that this hall was not a direct reference for the one in the Steiger House, at least as far as he was aware.

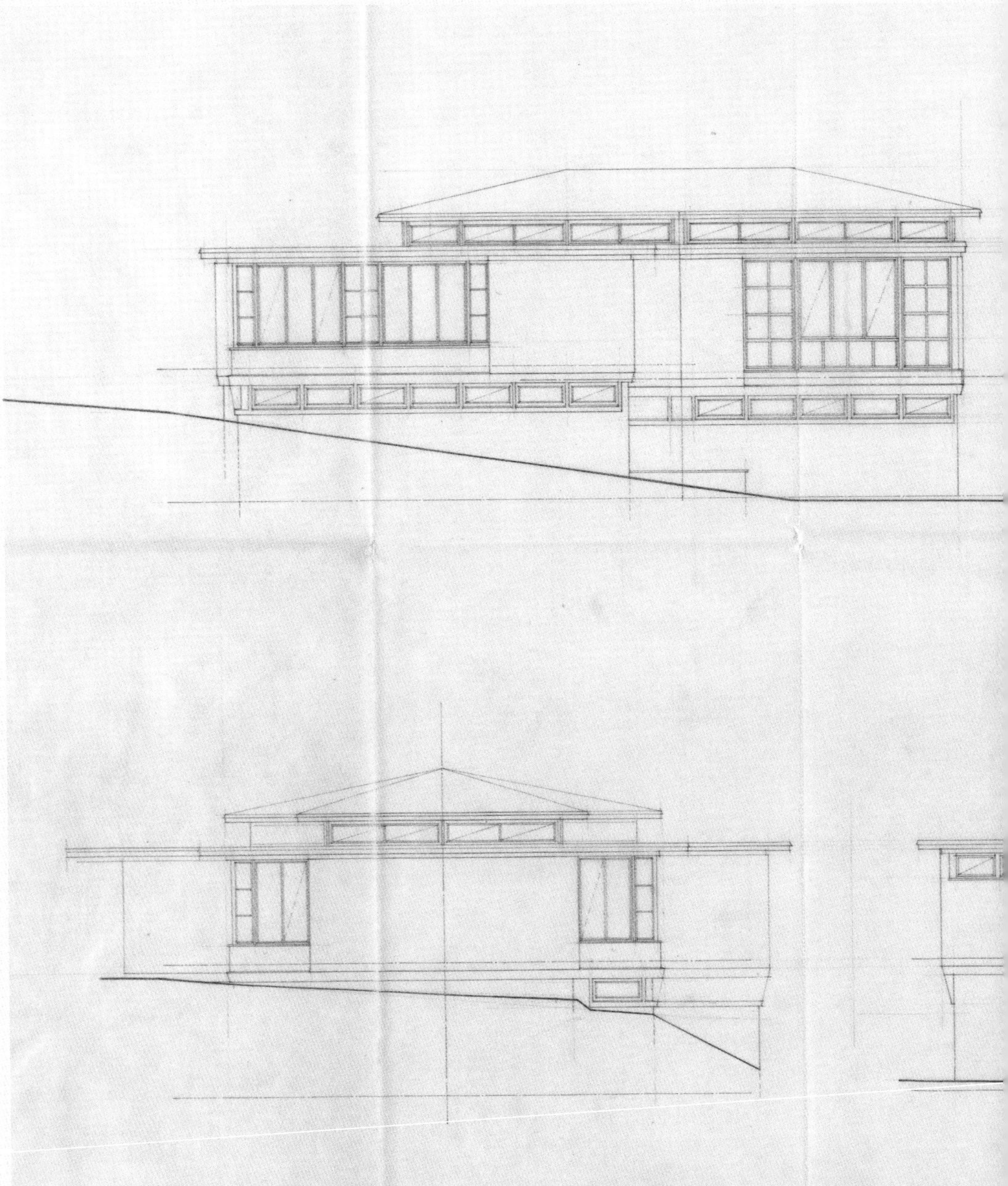

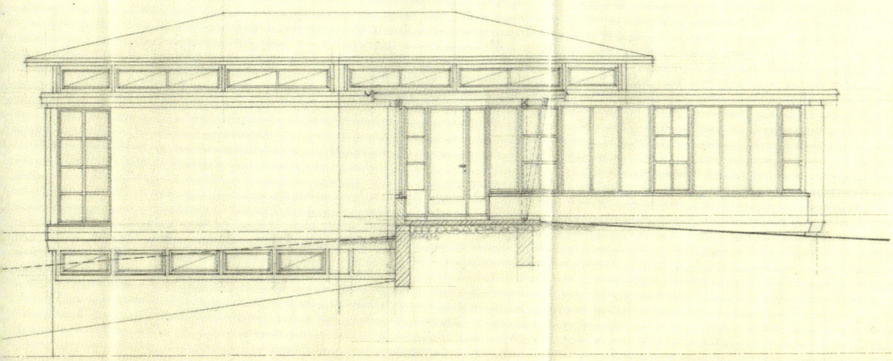

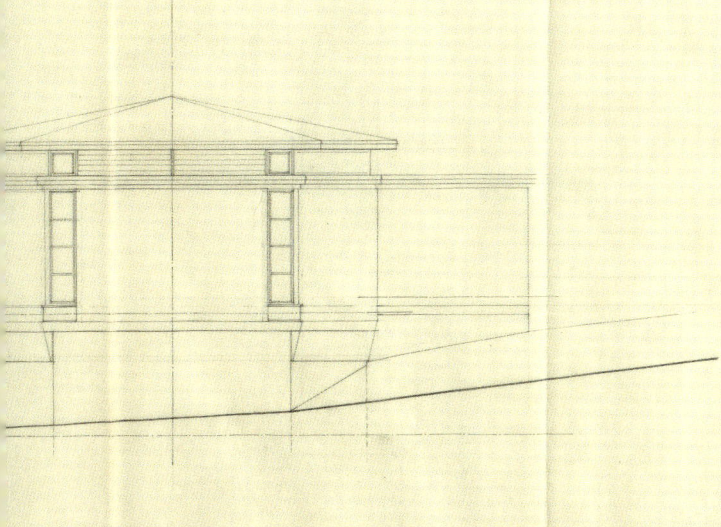

25 — Cf. Peter Steiger, *Chancen und Widerstände auf dem Weg zum nachhaltigen Planen und Bauen*, Zurich, gta Verlag, 2009, p. 263 f.

Photo (1993) by: Michel Zumbrunn

The balconies that run around the building act as a brise-soleil. In summer they provide shade to the glass facades. In winter, when the sun is low, light penetrates deep into the apartment.

This also helps maintain a comfortable temperature in the apartments during the rest of the year.
Photo (1993) by: Michel Zumbrunn

The studio of Flora Steiger-Crawford

Photo (1993) by: Michel Zumbrunn

Between Pilotis and Mushroom Columns

The Nuanced Articulated Structure of the Steiger-Crawford House

The house designed by Rudolf Steiger and Flora Steiger-Crawford evokes a sense of something "floating." The hallmark of its exterior is the horizontal articulation employed for the various floors, which is further underscored by the encircling cantilevered balconies. It is impossible to miss the two striking mushroom-shaped columns that frame the entrance and serve as characteristic components to transfer loads from the house above.(Fig. 1) The planning work for the Steiger-Crawford House's load-bearing structure was handled by engineering firm Fietz & Hauri, headed by Hans Rudolf Fietz and Hans H. Hauri.[26] The latter was subsequently appointed Professor of Structural Engineering and Construction at ETH Zurich (1963–1989) where he also served as President of the university (1968–1973).[27] Even the address on the plans, Zurich's prestigious *Bahnhofstrasse 24*, suggests that this was a very successful and well-respected engineering firm in post-war Switzerland.

(In-)visible Components

The development of the design for the Steiger-Crawford House reveals that the emphasis on the external horizontal articulation grew increasingly pronounced with each step in the design process, while the basic layout with a central floor plan was present from the outset (see Chronology on page 42). The floating effect that is the building's hallmark came into being as the horizontal elements of the load-bearing structure increasingly came to the fore, while its vertical elements were expressed with great restraint. It seems to have been clearly defined which architectural components were to be visible – and which were not. At first glance, the entire structural system appears much more uniform than is actually the case. It seems to be a relatively slender column-and-slab construction;[28] however, the house's structural system is actually much more dispersed. The primary structure is made up of various

Fig. 1 View from the east

The two striking Y-shaped columns create a mise-en-scène of the entrance and simultaneously of the load-bearing structure. All the other structural elements have a much more restrained appearance. Photo (1962) by: Walter Binder

types of columns, shear walls, and slabs. The positioning and articulation of these structural elements is primarily guided by the design, which is grounded in spatial relationships. In the rear sections, where the house is set into the slope, a more solid construction method was chosen, contrasting somewhat with the pared-down character of the rest of the structural system. This solid construction method does however make the basement rooms more usable and offers better bracing to absorb horizontal forces. The basement plays at best a – literally – subordinate role in the design, as reflected in Rudolf Steiger's decision, when the project was published in the *Schweizerische Bauzeitung* in 1963, not to show the portion of the structural system embedded in the ground, instead simply depicting this section with inconspicuous hatching.[29] The diversity of the structural system is also apparent in the choice of materials. Most of the load-bearing components are in reinforced concrete, including the slabs,(Fig. 5–6) some external walls, the large columns next to the entrance,(Fig. 2–3) and the foundations. Most of the interior walls, on the other hand, are made of brickwork. In addition, slim steel columns filled with concrete were also incorporated.(Fig. 4) As a result, the columns at the corners of the building appear very slender, while the facade's subtle division at the corners further "disguises" the existence of these columns; an indication that certain structural elements are intended to be "less visible."

Indirect Load Transfer

The functioning of the load transfer is deliberately obscured, as a comparison of the various levels reveals, even if only upon closer inspection. For example, the walls that run obliquely in the floor plan and mark out the recess in the middle of the facade are not directly supported by a wall or column below. That also holds true for the concrete-filled steel columns in the corners, which appear to float, as the large Y-shaped columns on the entrance level are set further back. As a result, the structural elements on the entrance level do not coincide directly with those on the floors above, as components like the oblique walls and the concrete-filled steel columns are not supported directly by the two Y-shaped columns, but rather by the 30-cm-thick slab. To make the structure appear leaner, an offset was created in the underside of the slab, which was also tapered towards the outer edges to make them as discreet as possible. As a result, the slab performs its feat of strength virtually imperceptibly. The slab above the entrance floor has a very high concentration of reinforcement compared to typical reinforced concrete slabs from this period. (Fig. 5), [30] In order to be able to absorb the large internal forces, mainly bending stresses, the upper layer of reinforcement consists of reinforcement bars with diameters of 22 mm (transverse) and 14 mm (longitudinal). The bottom layer even has reinforcement bars with diameters of 24 mm (transverse) and 16 mm (longitudinal). In comparison, reinforcement bars with diameters of 12 to 14 mm were conventionally used at the time. The high degree of reinforcement is also evident in the very close meshing in certain areas where the reinforcement bars are placed at intervals of only 10 cm. (Fig. 5)

Between Pilotis and Mushroom Columns

The generally inconspicuous structural elements emphasize the essential idea inspiring the design, which is grounded in perception of the visual relationships between the rooms, as well as between interior and exterior. While the structural function of most of the components is thus not fully visible, the expressive Y-shaped columns flanking the entrance are an exception. In this case, the load-bearing structure is not concealed, but staged, as the sculptural form of the columns makes clear. The design process reveals that very different solutions were analyzed, including slanted walls in the floor plan, pillars with cantilevered supports above, and V-shaped columns. The Y-shaped solution that was ultimately chosen appears very distinctive and at the same time somewhat unconventional, as the three wings of the columns do not share the same geometry. (Fig. 2) In addition, a more marked paring down, ensuring fewer edges on the underside, would probably have rendered the column's shape even more expressive. Overall, the two columns represent a fascinating hybrid combining pilotis and mushroom columns, two important

26 — Portrait of engineering firm Fietz & Hauri: Werner Jegher, "Ingenieurbüro Rolf Fietz, vormals Fietz & Hauri," in: *Schweizerische Bauzeitung*, 87, 8, 1969, pp. 132–133.

27 — Cf. "Hans Hauri," in: *ETH History 1855–2005*, https://www.ethistory.ethz.ch/rueckblicke/hochschulgremien/alumni/weitere_seiten/4_8_hauri/popupfriendly. 2005.

28 — On the definition of column-and-slab structures cf. Heino Engel, *Tragsysteme / Structure Systems*, 5th edition, Ostfildern, 1997, pp. 50 f. and 207.

29 — Cf. Rudolf Steiger, "Haus Steiger an der Bergstrasse in Zürich," in: *Schweizerische Bauzeitung*, 81, 33, 1963, pp. 590–591.

30 — On the load-bearing behavior of reinforced concrete slabs cf. Joseph Schwartz, "Tragwerksentwurf II", script, ETH Zurich, Department of Architecture, 2011, pp. 39–42. https://block.arch.ethz.ch/eq/files/SchwartzSkriptTE_1_2_1507219782.pdf

formal and structural concepts of twentieth-century modern architecture. Pilotis are an integral part of the vocabulary of modernism, especially since Le Corbusier counted the slender columns at entrance level among *"Les cinq points d'une architecture nouvelle" (Five Points of Architecture)*.[31] In Haefeli Moser Steiger's work, this concept can often be found in very different formulations, for example in the renowned Rotach houses (1927–1928) or the commercial building "Zur Palme" (1955–1964) in Zurich. The influence of the mushroom column, which stems more from a technical, engineering background, is more surprising. The system was developed in the early twentieth century to strengthen the novel beamless slabs made of reinforced concrete in warehouse buildings, which were designed for high loads.[32] In Europe, Robert Maillart was instrumental in researching and disseminating this principle;[33] his pendant in the United States was Claude Allen Porter Turner.[34] However, the combination selected for the Steiger-Crawford House – or rather the choice of mushroom columns instead of pilotis – is unorthodox and rather rare. Designs incorporating similar Y-shaped columns, which however cantilever even further, can be found, for instance, in the works of the Italian engneers Pier Luigi Nervi[35] and Sergio Musmeci.[36] The Steiger-Crawford House is an interesting example of a design in which the load-bearing structure plays a crucial role without appearing obtrusive as a whole. While most of the architecture's feats of strength remain concealed, the striking columns refer to a heightened formal expression of the flow of forces.

31 — Werner Oechslin, "Les Cinq Points d'une Architecture Nouvelle", in: *Assemblage*, 4, 1987, pp. 82–93.

32 — On the development of beamless slabs made of reinforced concrete, cf. Andreas Thuy, *Unterzuglose Decken. Konstruktionskulturen des Eisenbetons anhand von "Flat Slabs" und Pilzdecken in den USA, der Schweiz und dem Deutschen Reich im Spannungsfeld der Triade aus Unternehmertum, Wissenschaft und Regulierung 1904–1929*, Diss., ETH Zurich, Department of Architecture, 2023.

33 — Cf. Armand Fürst and Peter Marti, "Robert Maillart's Design Approach for Flat Slabs," in: *ASCE Journal of Structural Engineering*, 123, 8, 1997, pp. 1102–1110.

34 — Cf. Dario Gasparini, "Contributions of C.A.P. Turner to Development of Reinforced Concrete Flat Slabs 1905–1909," in: *ASCE Journal of Structural Engineering*, 128, 10, 2002, pp. 1243–1252.

35 — The Italian Embassy in Brasília (1969–1977) should be highlighted in this context. Cf. Tullia Iori and Sergio Poretti, *Pier Luigi Nervi. L'Ambasciata d'Italia a Brasilia*, Milan, 2008, pp. 90–91.

36 — These include the Edificio degli Assessorati of the Palazzo della Regione in Trento (1953–1966), the Palazzine in Via Vallombrosa in Rome (1958–1959), as well as the Albergo Castello in Martina Franca (1973, not completed). Cf. Lukas Ingold, *Form as the Unknown. Sergio Musmeci – Explorations in the Design of Structures*, Diss., ETH Zurich, Department of Architecture, 2021, pp. 202, 212 f., 441 and 453.

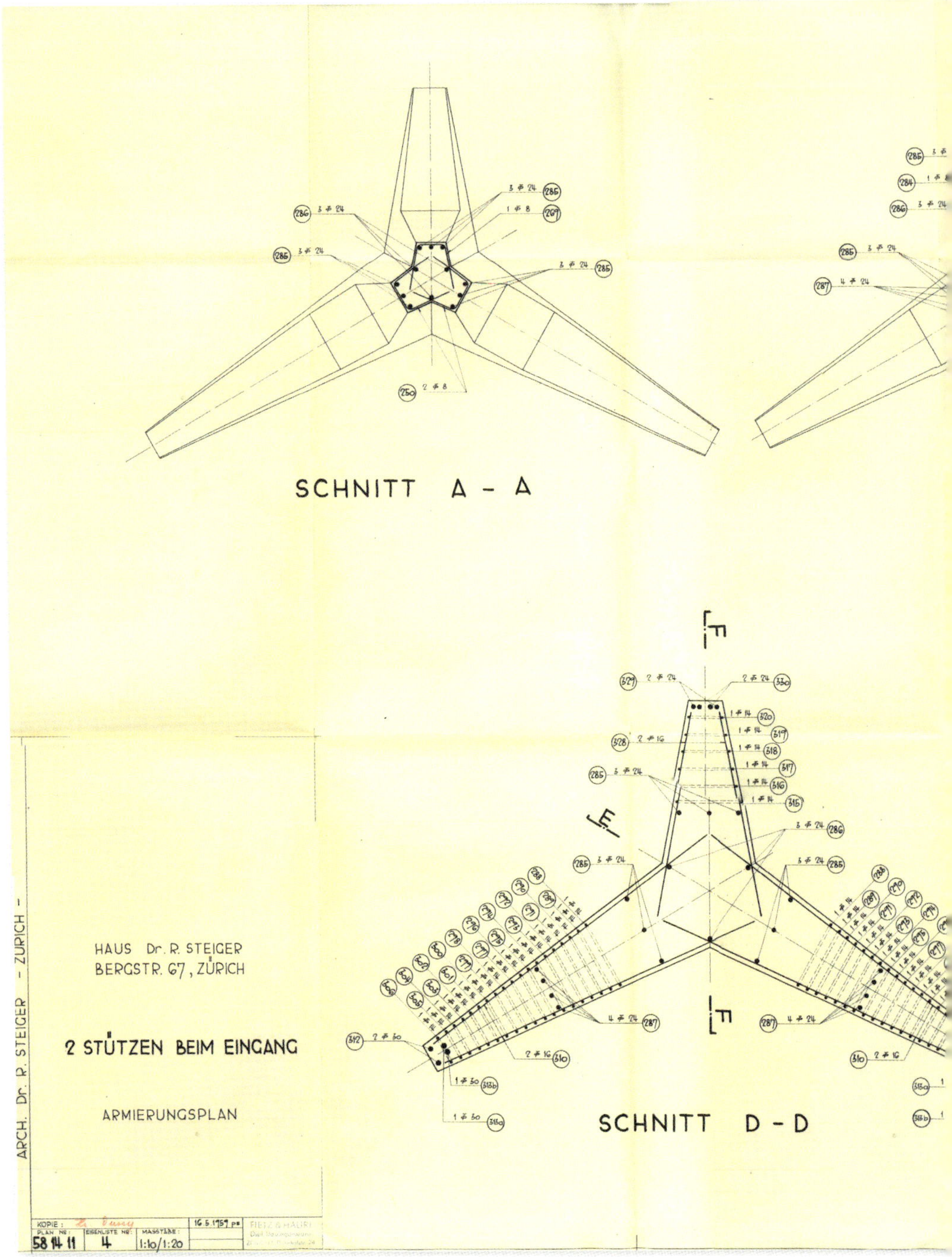
SCHNITT A - A
SCHNITT D - D
HAUS Dr. R. STEIGER
BERGSTR. 67, ZÜRICH
2 STÜTZEN BEIM EINGANG
ARMIERUNGSPLAN
ARCH. Dr. R. STEIGER - ZÜRICH -
KOPIE:
PLAN NR: 58 14 11
EISENLISTE NR: 4
MASSTÄBE: 1:10/1:20
16.5.1959

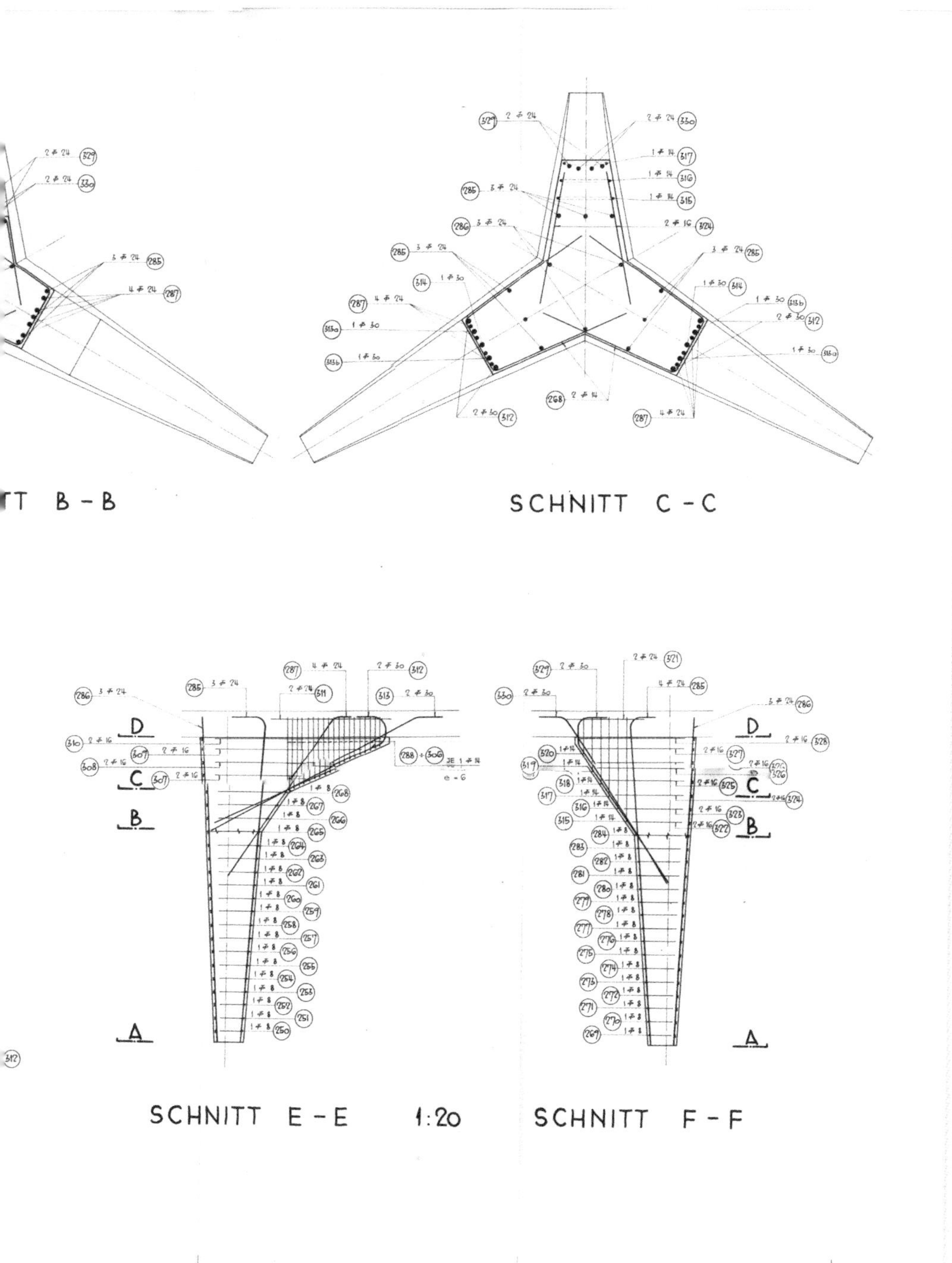

Fig. 2 Plan of Y-shaped columns

The reinforcement bars at the edges have diameters of up to 30 mm.
They are primarily subjected to compressive forces and thus ensure the vertical load transfer.

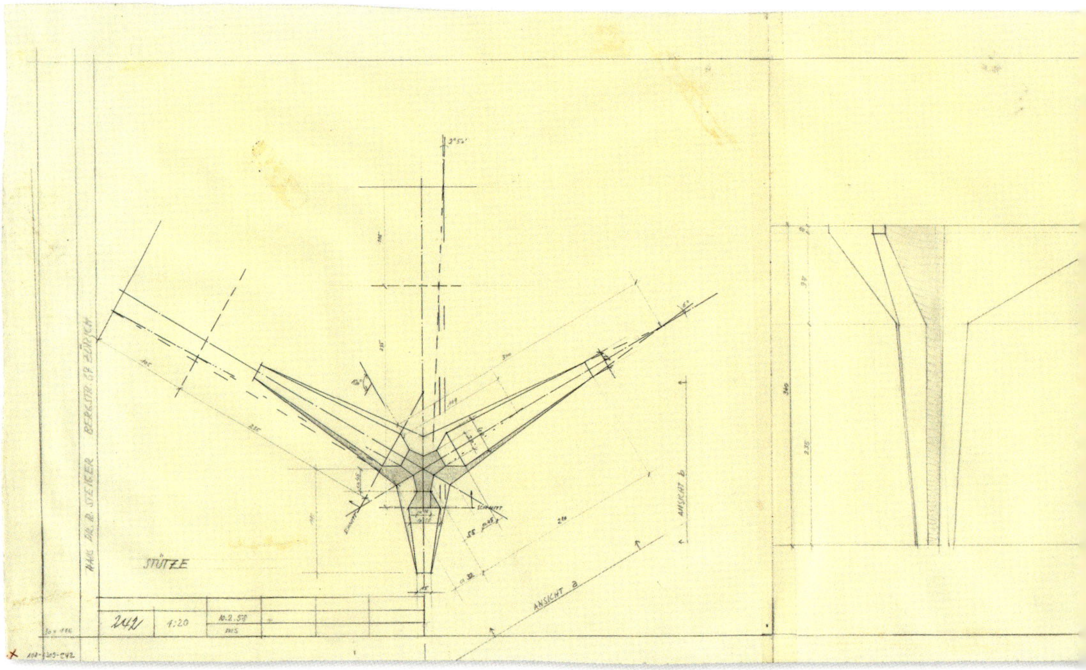
STÜTZE
1:20
ANSICHT a
ANSICHT b

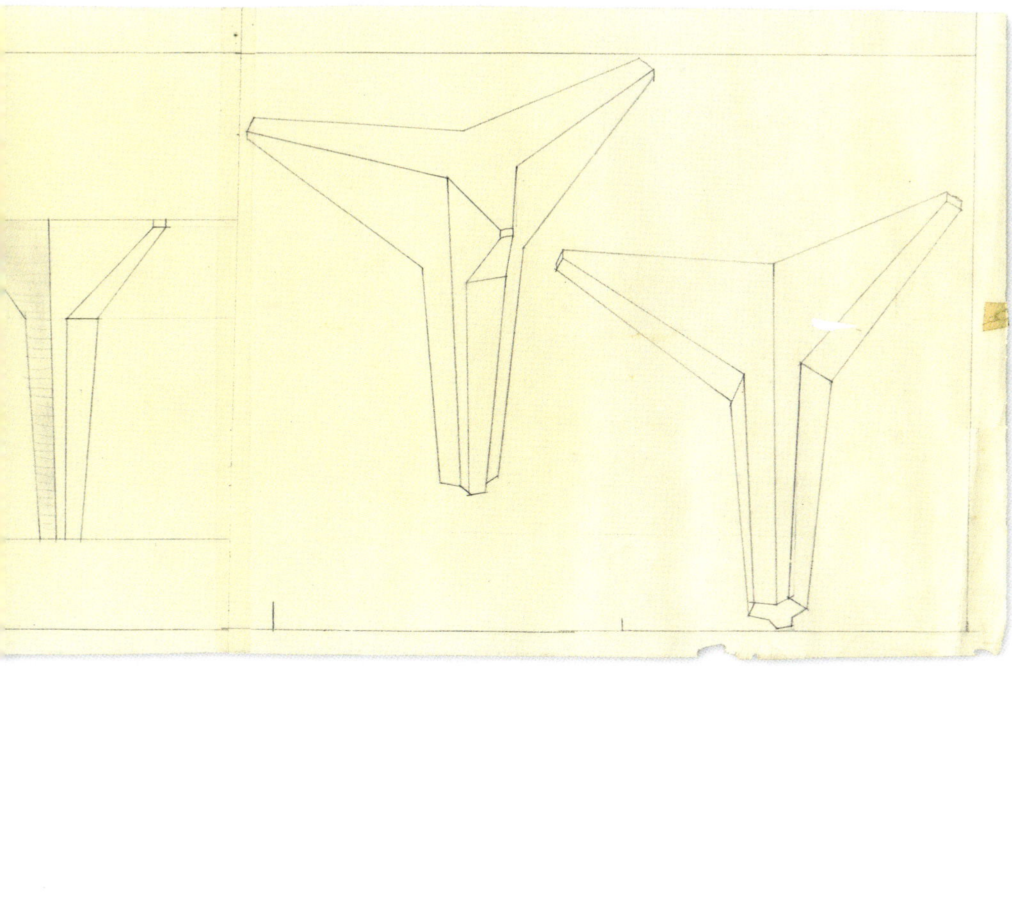

Fig. 3 Bottom and side views of Y-shaped column

The studies show a slightly simplified form. In contrast to the executed version, the undersides of the long wings are straight here.

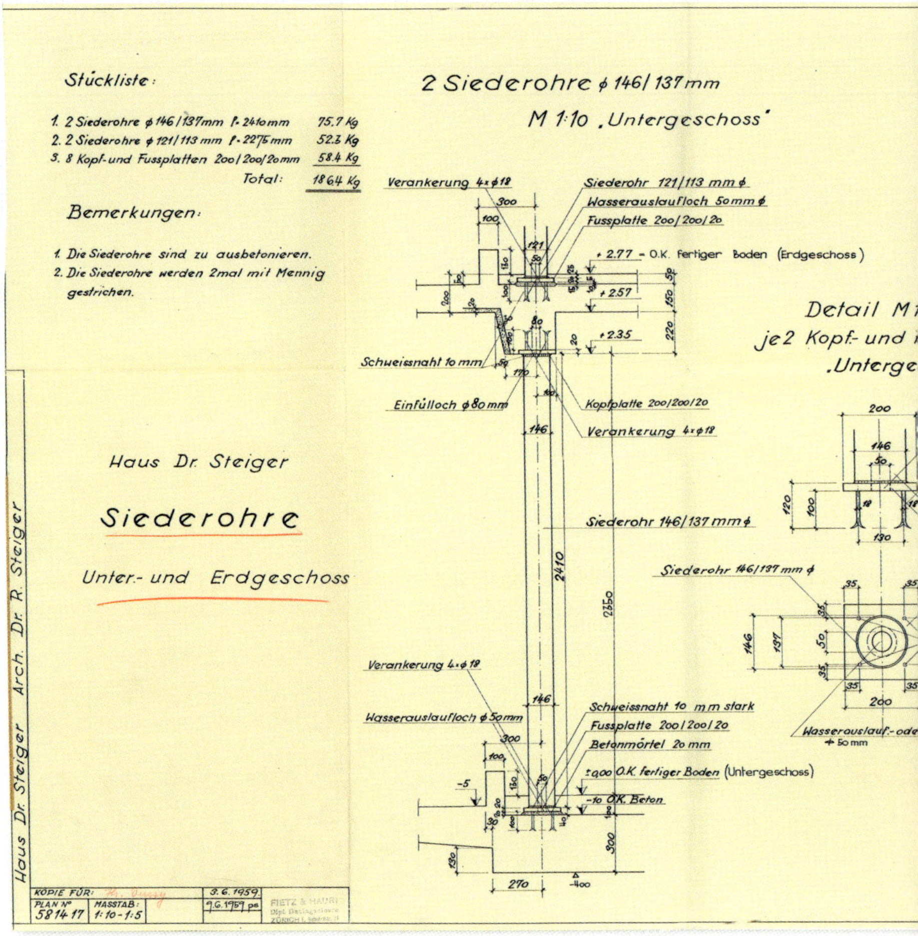

Stückliste:
1. 2 Siederohre ϕ 146/137mm l=2410mm 75.7 Kg
2. 2 Siederohre ϕ 121/113 mm l=2275mm 52.3 Kg
3. 8 Kopf- und Fussplatten 200/200/20mm 58.4 Kg
Total: 186.4 Kg
Bemerkungen:
1. Die Siederohre sind zu ausbetonieren.
2. Die Siederohre werden 2mal mit Mennig gestrichen.
Haus Dr. Steiger
Siederohre
Unter.- und Erdgeschoss
Haus Dr. Steiger Arch. Dr. R. Steiger
2 Siederohre ϕ 146/137mm
M 1:10 „Untergeschoss"
Verankerung 4×ϕ18
Siederohr 121/113 mm ϕ
Wasserauslaufloch 50mm ϕ
Fussplatte 200/200/20
+2.77 = O.K. fertiger Boden (Erdgeschoss)
+2.57
+2.35
Schweissnaht 10 mm
Einfülloch ϕ80mm
Kopfplatte 200/200/20
Verankerung 4×ϕ18
Siederohr 146/137 mmϕ
Verankerung 4×ϕ18
Wasserauslaufloch ϕ50mm
Schweissnaht 10 mm stark
Fussplatte 200/200/20
Betonmörtel 20 mm
±0.00 O.K. fertiger Boden (Untergeschoss)
-10 O.K. Beton
Detail M
je2 Kopf- und
.Unterge
Siederohr 146/137 mm ϕ
Wasserauslauf.- ode
KOPIE FÜR:
PLAN Nº 581417
MASSTAB: 1:10-1:5
3.6.1959
9.6.1959
FIETZ & HAURI
ZÜRICH

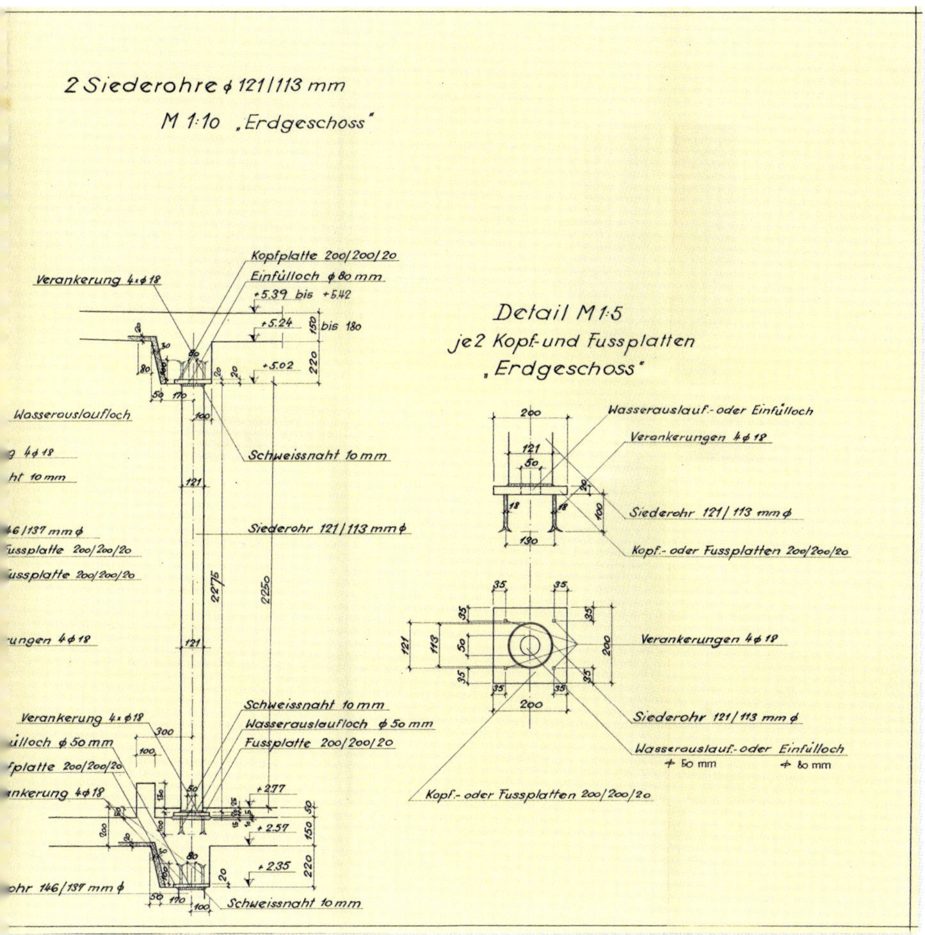

Fig. 4 Plan of concrete-filled steel columns

The steel tubes have diameters of just 121 mm and 146 mm respectively. These slender pipes were filled with concrete.

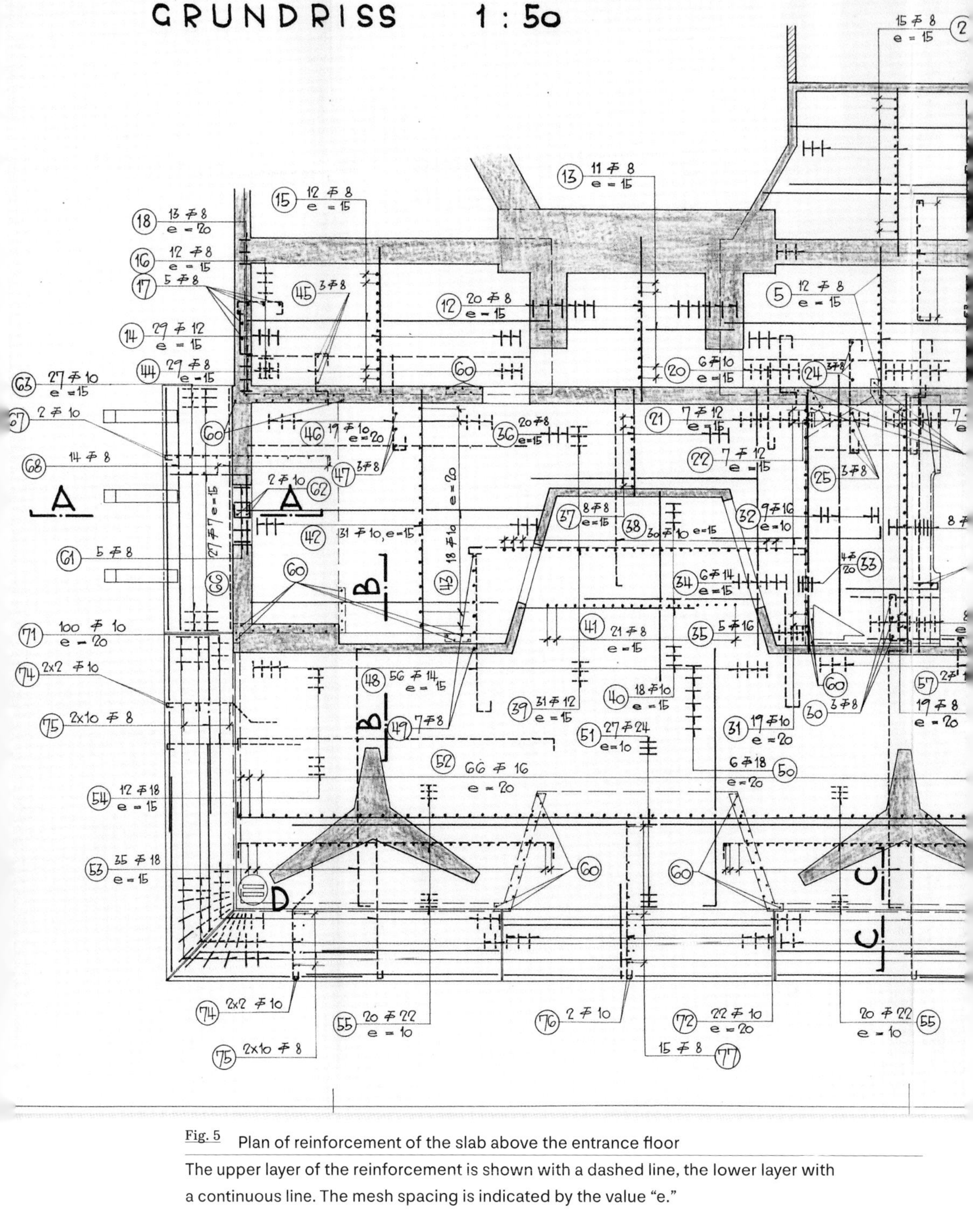

Fig. 5 Plan of reinforcement of the slab above the entrance floor

The upper layer of the reinforcement is shown with a dashed line, the lower layer with a continuous line. The mesh spacing is indicated by the value “e.”

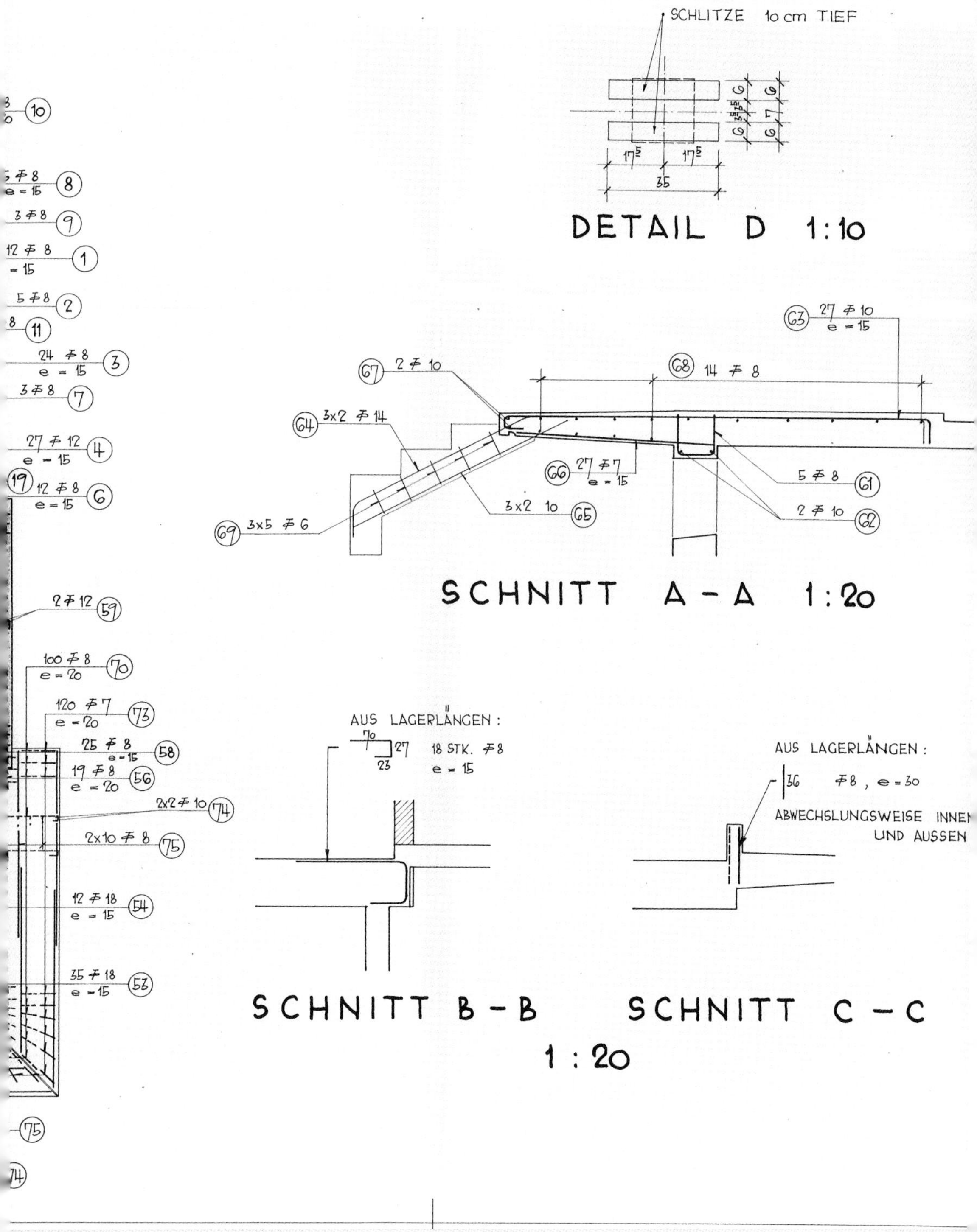

Fig. 6 **Next page:** Plan of reinforcement of the slab between the residential floors

The slab between the two upper floors has a significantly lower amount of reinforcement, mainly because it does not have to absorb any offsets from the vertical load transfer.

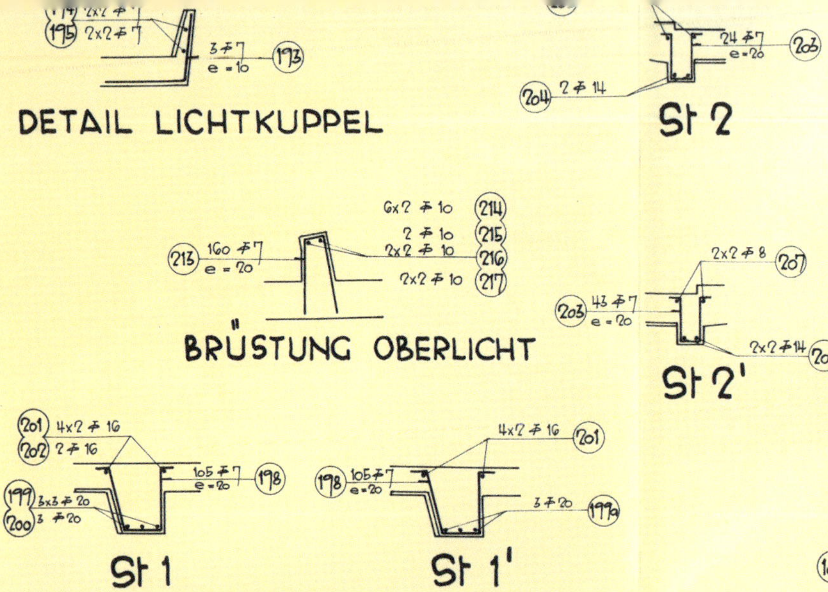

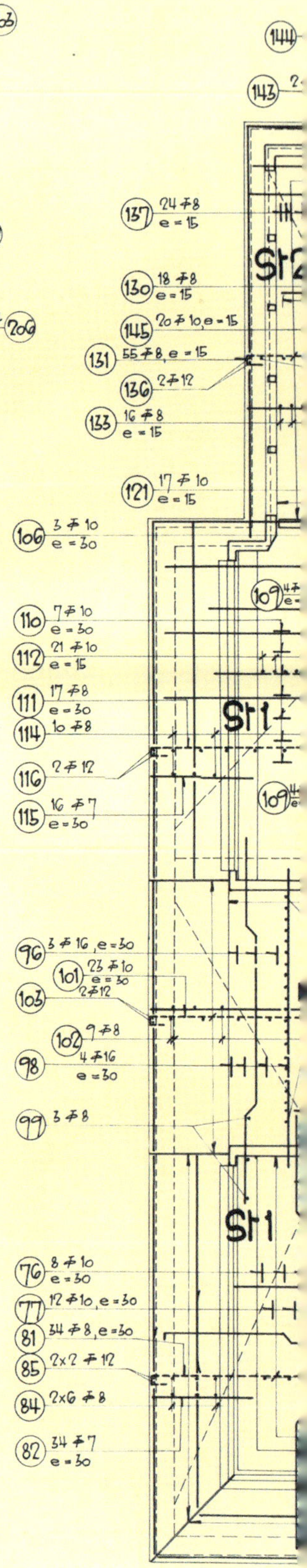

ARCH. Dr. R. STEIGER – ZÜRICH –

HAUS Dr. R. STEIGER
BERGSTR. 67, ZÜRICH

DECKE ÜBER ERDGESCHOSS

ARMIERUNGSPLAN

AUSFÜHRUNG
EXECUTION

POS. 218 (108 ∓ 16) = ANSCHLUSS-EISEN FÜR PFEILER IM OBERLICHT !

KOPIE FÜR:			23. 7. 1959 DG
PLAN No. 58 14 27	MASSTÄBE 1:20/1:50	EISENLISTE No. 15	

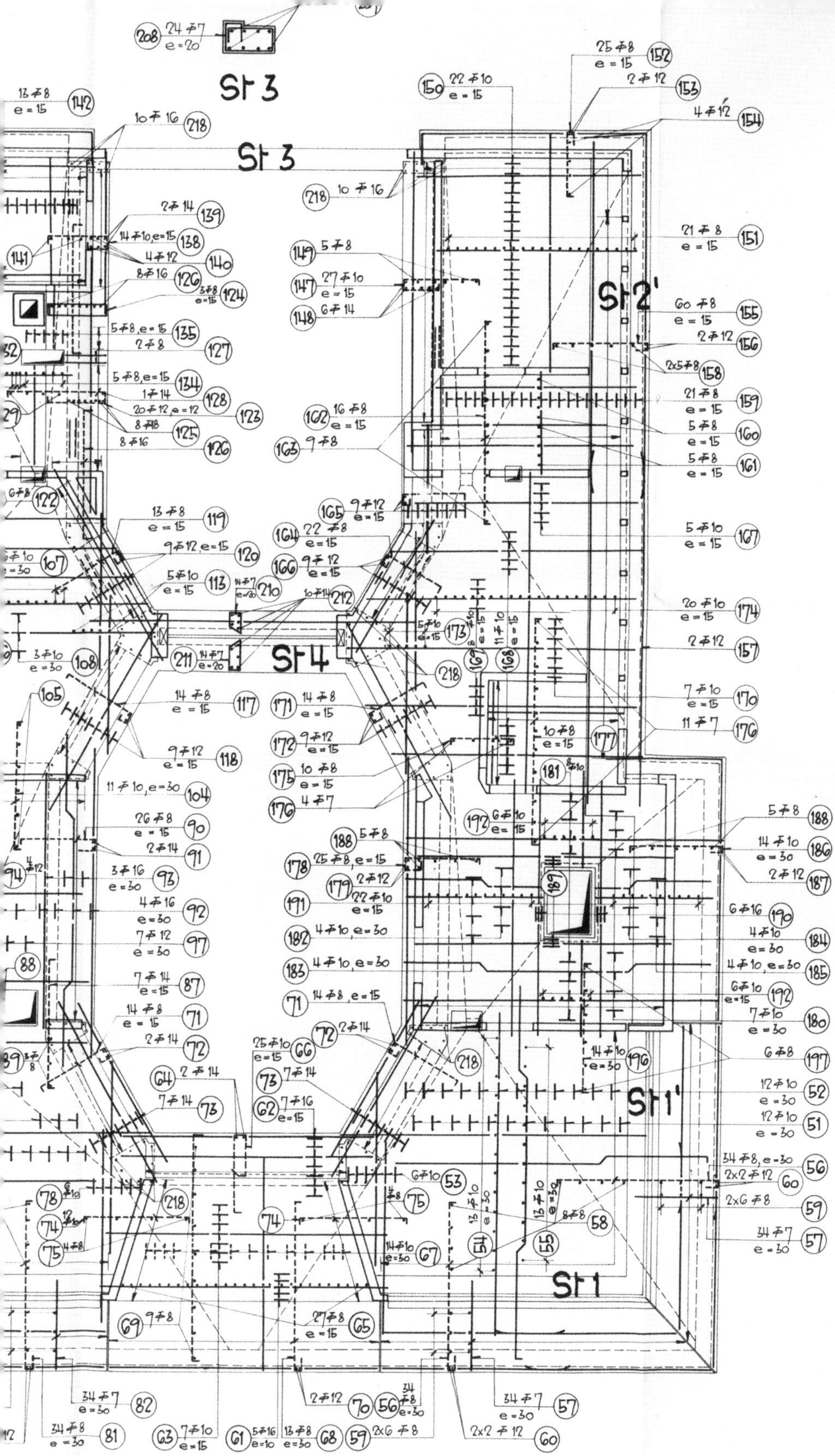

St 3
St 3
St 2'
St 4
St 1'
St 1

Photo (1993) by: Michel Zumbrunn

Photo (1993) by: Michel Zumbrunn

Construction and Tectonics

Building Envelope

The perceptions of the building from Bergstrasse "coming up" or from the valley "coming down" are fundamentally different; in one case it looks like a cube, while on the other hand it looks like an upright front-end building with a stairwell set back towards the slope and an elongated utility section.

The main facade is characterized by a view of the underside of the pronounced overhanging roof, along with the two balconies encircling the building, encompassing massive protruding shutter boxes that run round the corners. The two floors are "carried" by two sculpturally articulated pillars in front of the rear wall with the recessed entrance. The balcony layer is indicated in the underside of the ceiling above the entrance by a small offset as a kind of load-bearing panel.

The building envelope consists of a double-skin construction[37] with an outer load-bearing exposed concrete wall and an inner brick wall. The ceilings and the cantilevered perimeters of the balconies are continuous, in other words not separated from the floor slab. The thermal bridges are "absorbed" on the inside with a cork strip. The floor-to-ceiling windows in the corner rooms are made of laminated glass, the small corner room windows are single-glazed, and the window strips on the northeast side with laminated glass. The roof water is drained into the waste-water shafts.

The constructive dispositive largely generates the tectonic image, including the expression of the facades:

The alternation of windows hinged on the inside and outside results in different reveal depths and thus different shadow patterns in contrast to the smooth glass facades of modernism.

The glazing in the corner rooms is spatially framed with overpanels and joists or shutter boxes and convectors, in contrast to modernist floor-to-ceiling glazing.

The small-scale corner glazing frames the free-standing, round steel support and emphasizes the corners of the room or the facades, in contrast to modernist style, which moved away from glass corners.[38]

The selection of details – layered sections in plan and cross section – show the construction of the building envelope as a transition between inside and outside and refer to the tectonic features of the building.[39]

37 — The construction and use of materials as implemented diverges in part from the plans, for example cork is used instead of Sagex (polystyrene foam) or laminated glass instead of double glazing, etc.

38 — The formation of corner glazing plays an important role in the assessment of modernism. Drawing on the evolution of the corner glazing in Walter Gropius' Bauhaus, in 1955, Colin Rowe and Robert Slutzky developed their essay on plurivalent space "Transparency. Literal and Phenomenal" (first published in *Perspecta*, 8, 1963, pp. 45–54); see also the German edition with a commentary by Bernhard Hoesli: Colin Rowe and Robert Slutzky, *Transparenz (Le Corbusier Studien, 1, Geschichte und Theorie der Architektur,* 4), Basel et al, Birkhäuser Verlag, 1968.

39 — Comparable studies include Christian Sumi and Ernst Strebel, "Detailzeichnungen," in *O. R. Salvisberg. Die andere Moderne*, ed. ETH Zurich, Zurich, gta Verlag, 1985, pp. 230–243; Marco Pogacnik, "Details. Architecture Seen in Section," in *IUAV*, 140, 2014, p. 1.

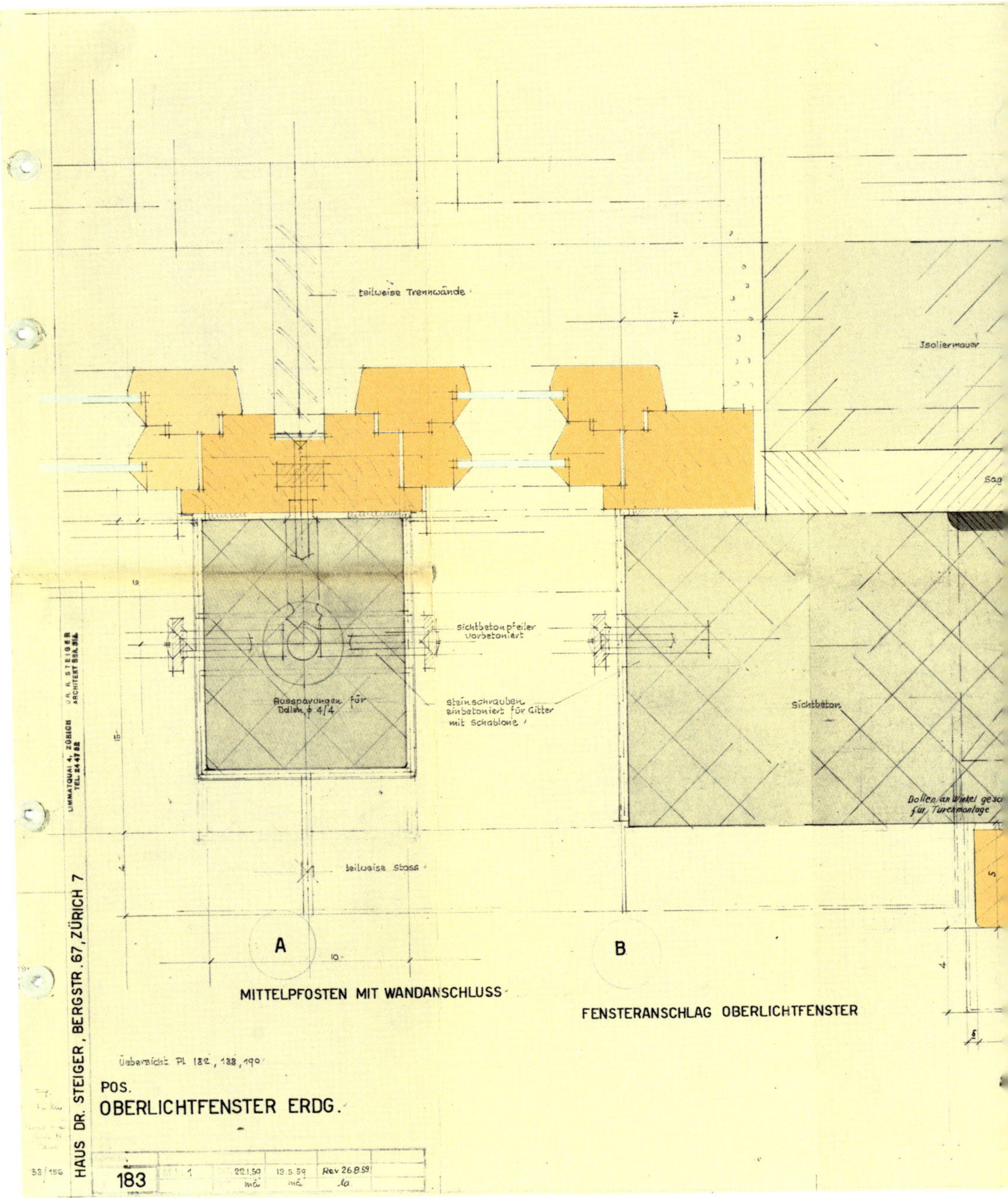

Skylight windows, ground floor, section

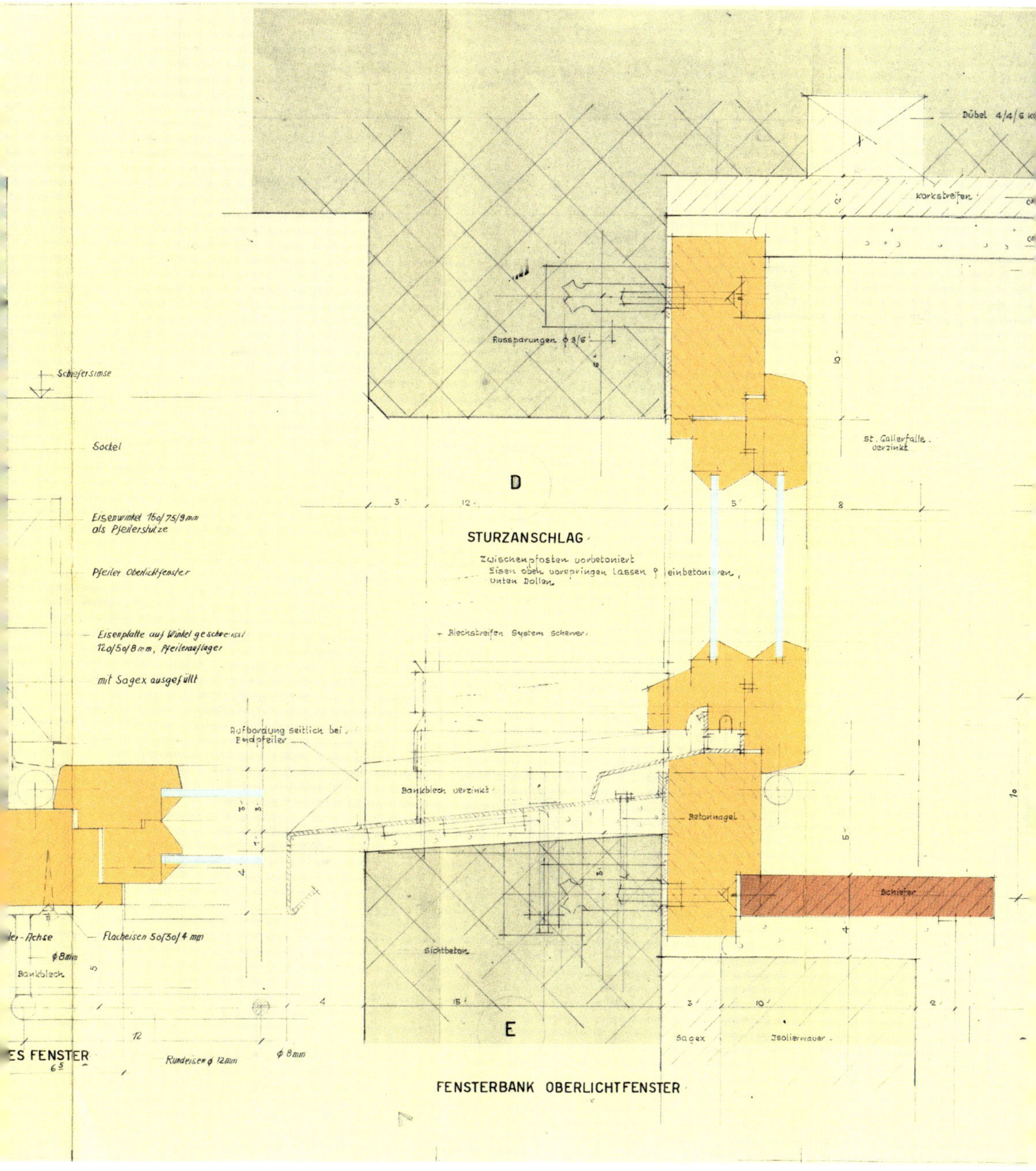

FENSTERBANK OBERLICHTFENSTER

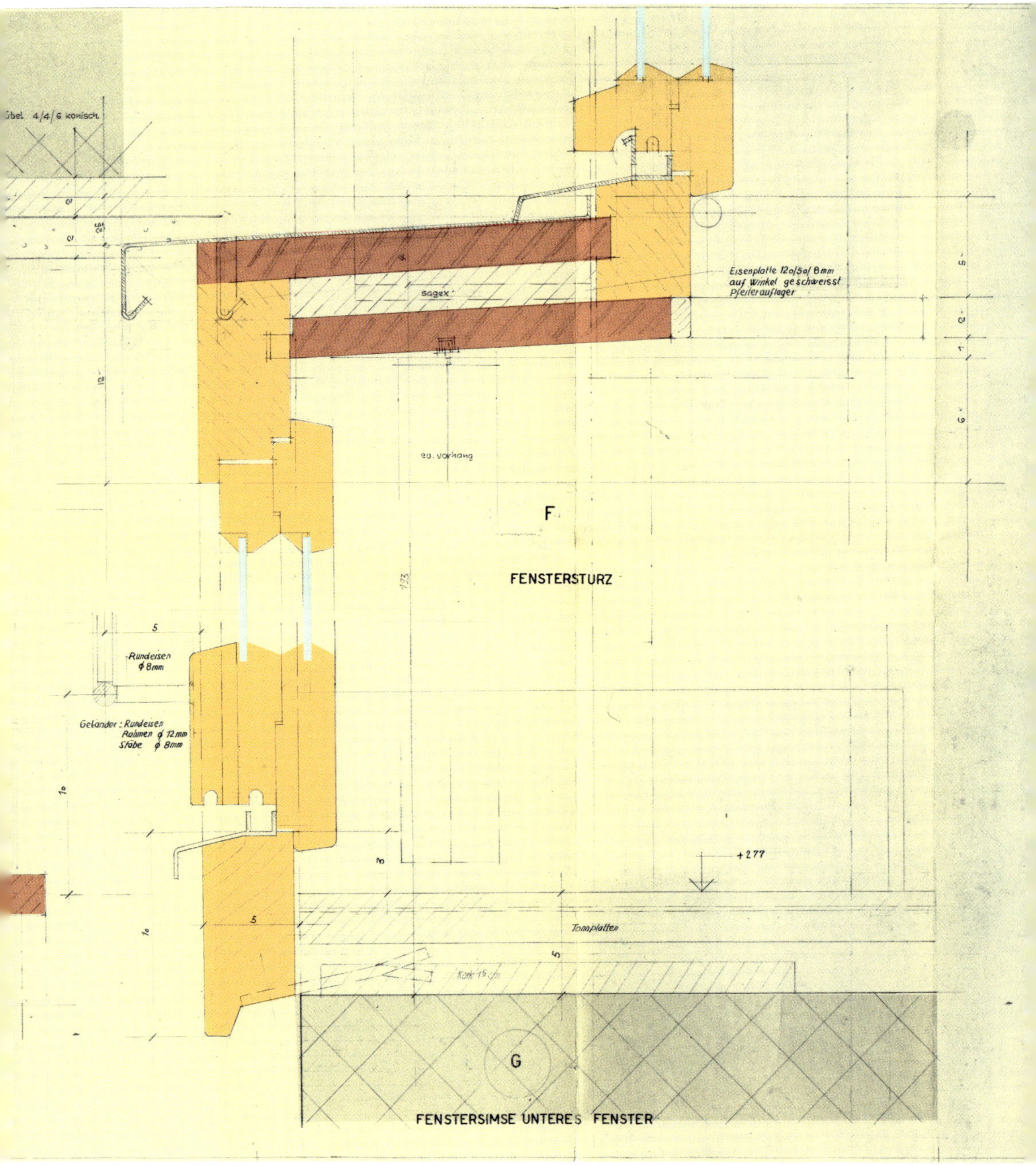

Garden door and window, section

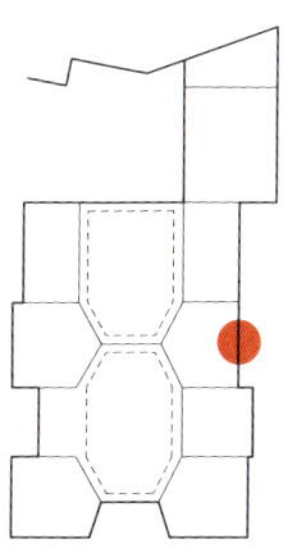

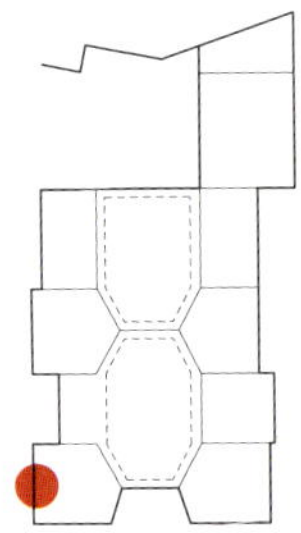

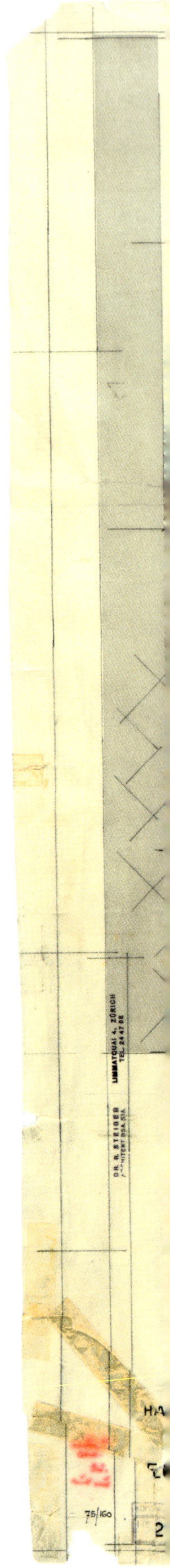

Sliding windows, ground floor

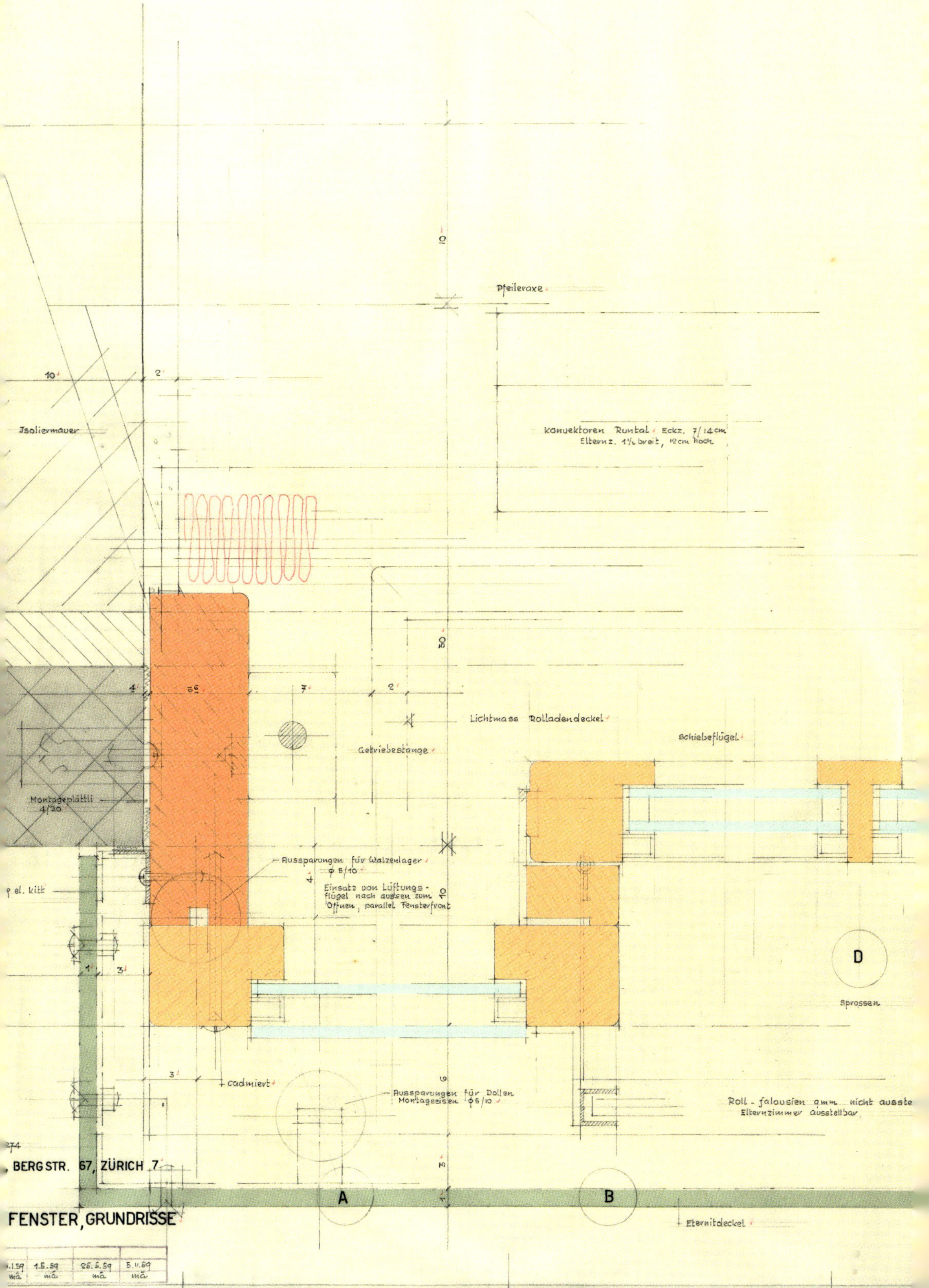

274

BERGSTR. 67, ZÜRICH 7

FENSTER, GRUNDRISSE

.1.59 mä	1.5.59 mä	26.5.59 mä	5.11.59 mä

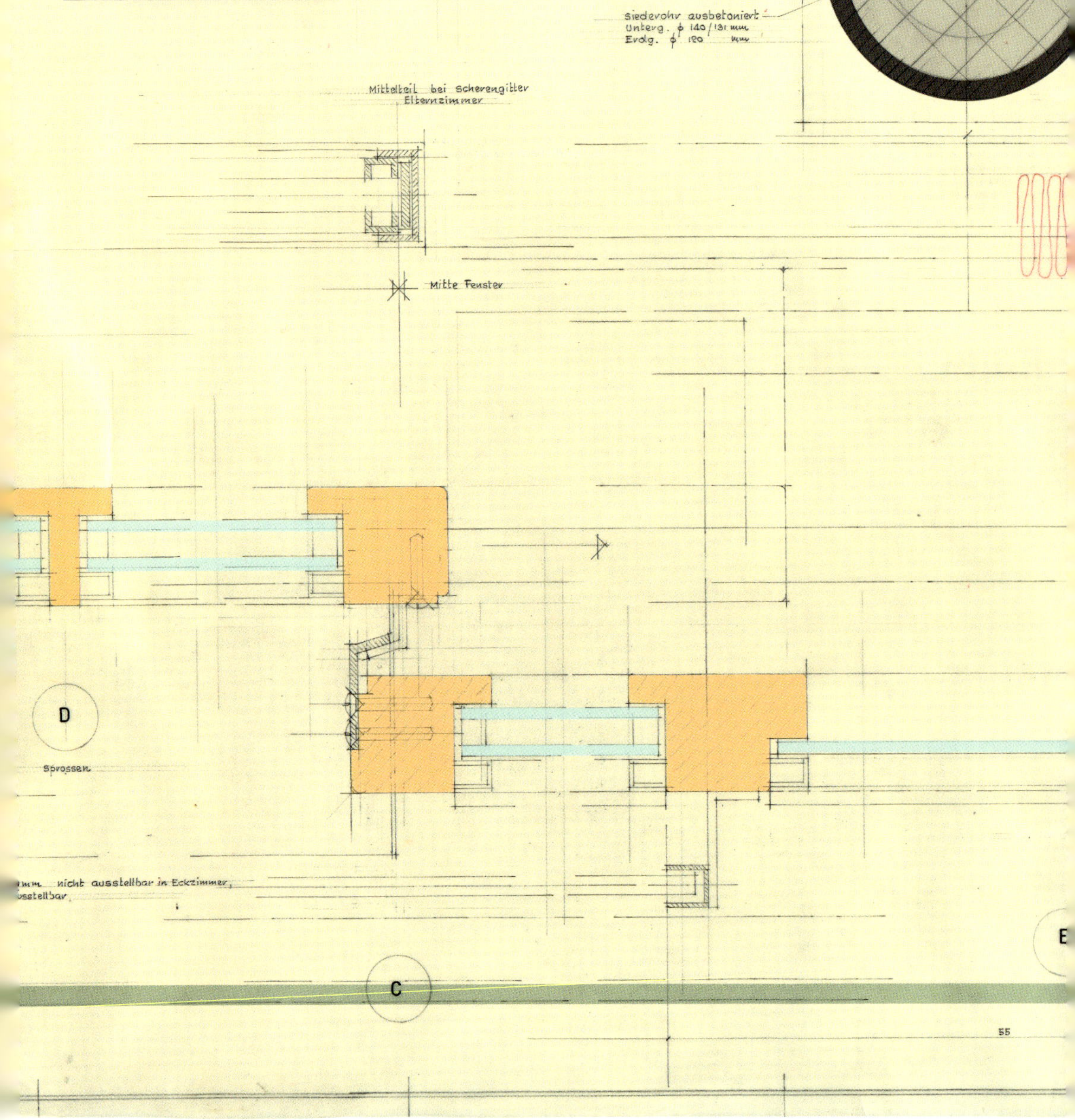

Betoneinfülloch
Loch unten für Ausdunstung Wasser
Siederohr ausbetoniert
Unterg. ϕ 140/131 mm
Erdg. ϕ 120 mm
Mittelteil bei Scherengitter
Elternzimmer
Mitte Fenster
D
Sprossen
mm nicht ausstellbar in Eckzimmer,
usstellbar
C
E

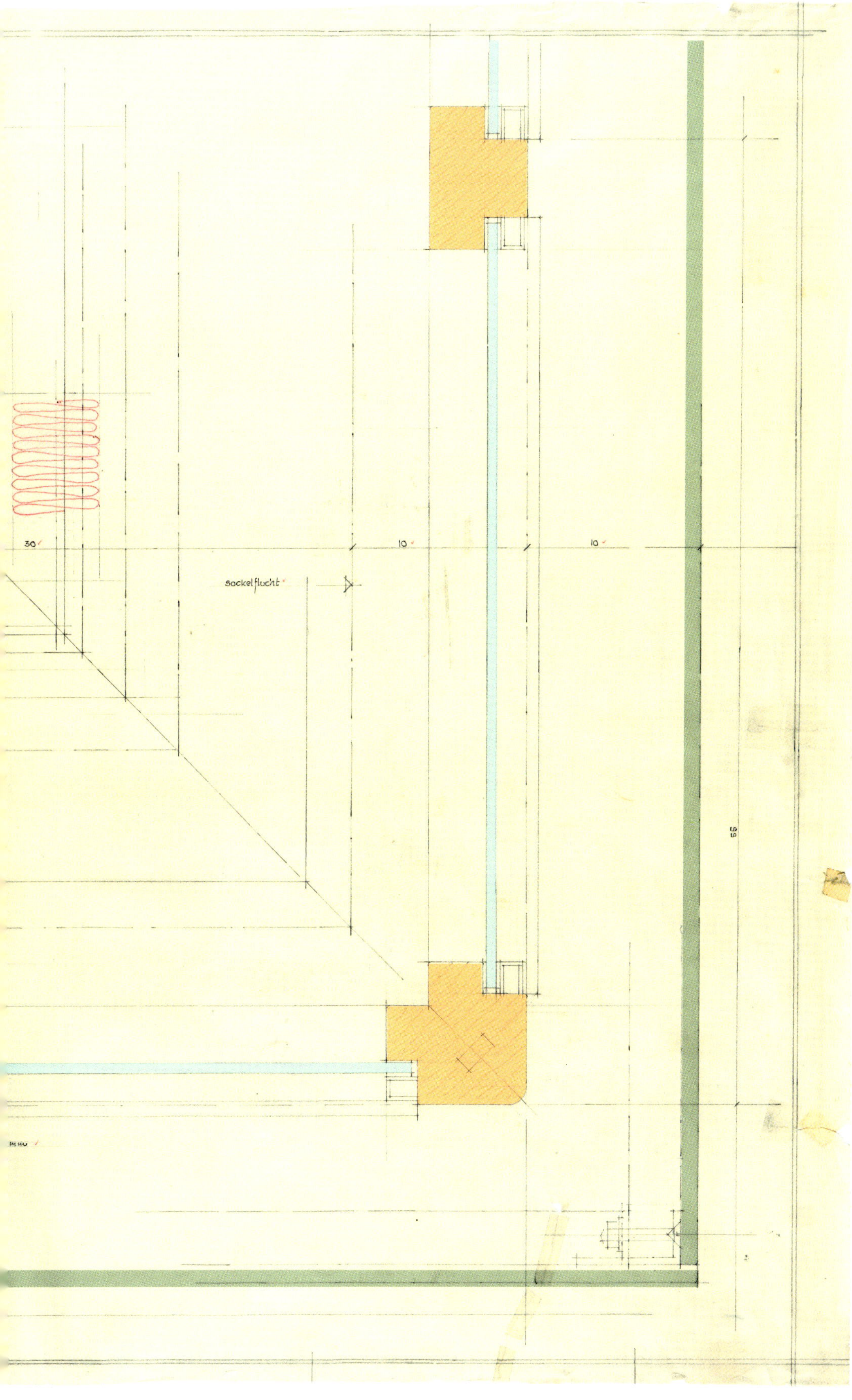

30
10
10
sockelflucht

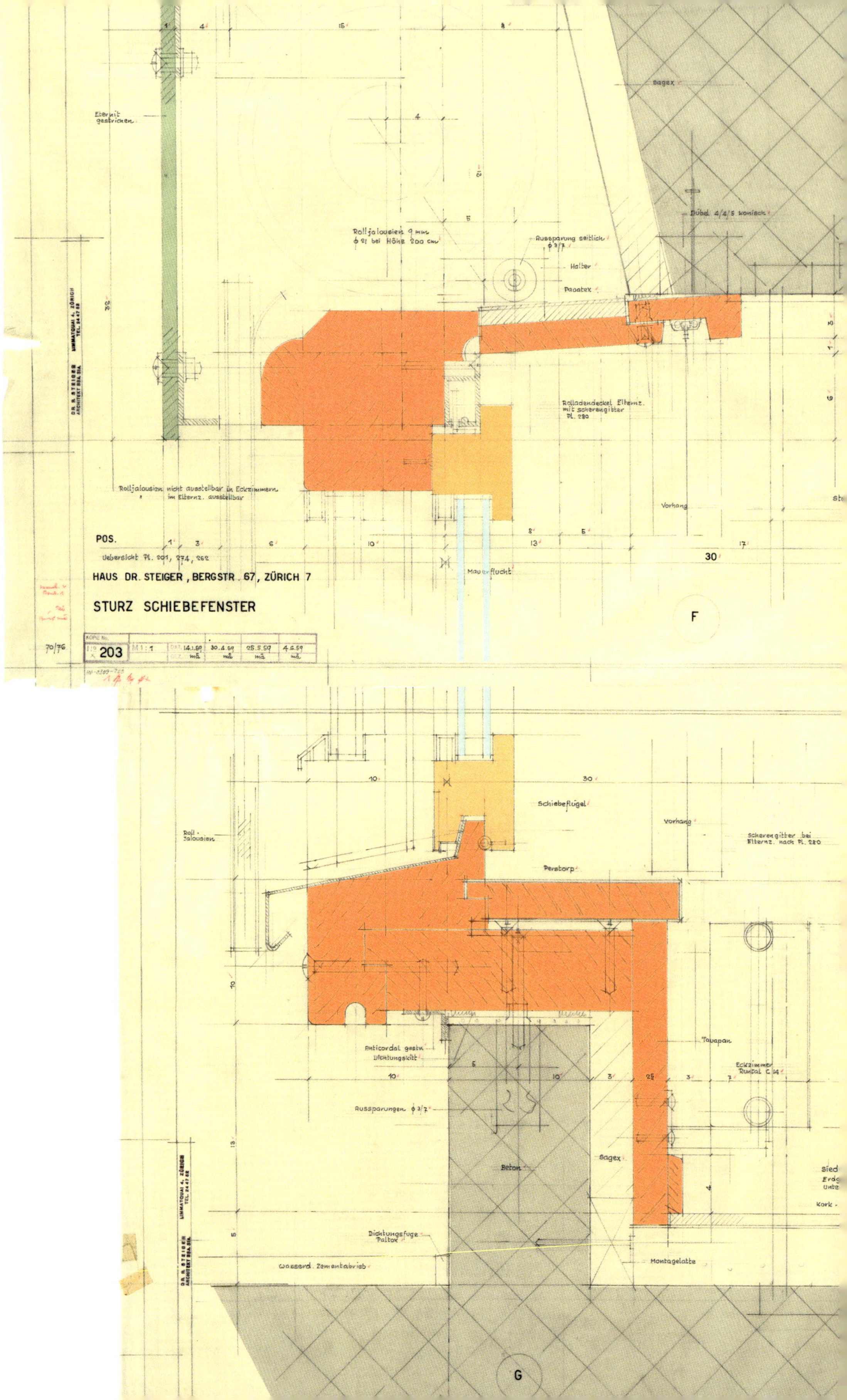

Eternit gestrichen
Sagex
Dübel 4/4/5 konisch
Rolljalousien 9 mm
φ 21 bei Höhe 200 cm
Aussparung seitlich φ 3/7
Halter
Pavatex
Rolladendeckel Elternz. mit Scherengitter Pl. 220
Rolljalousien nicht ausstellbar in Eckzimmern
im Elternz. ausstellbar
Vorhang
POS.
Uebersicht Pl. 201, 274, 262
HAUS DR. STEIGER, BERGSTR. 67, ZÜRICH 7
STURZ SCHIEBEFENSTER
Mauerflucht
F
203
M 1:1
14.1.59
30.4.59
25.5.59
4.6.59
DR. R. STEIGER ARCHITEKT BSA SIA LIMMATQUAI 4, ZÜRICH TEL. 24 47 82
Schiebeflügel
Vorhang
Roll-Jalousien
Scherengitter bei Elternz. nach Pl. 220
Perstorp
Anticordal gestr.
Dichtungskitt
Tavapan
Eckzimmer Runtal C 14
Aussparungen φ 3/7
Beton
Sagex
Dichtungsfuge Paltox
Montagelatte
Wasserd. Zementabrieb
G

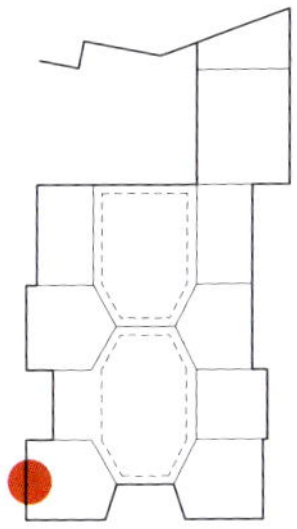

Sliding window, section

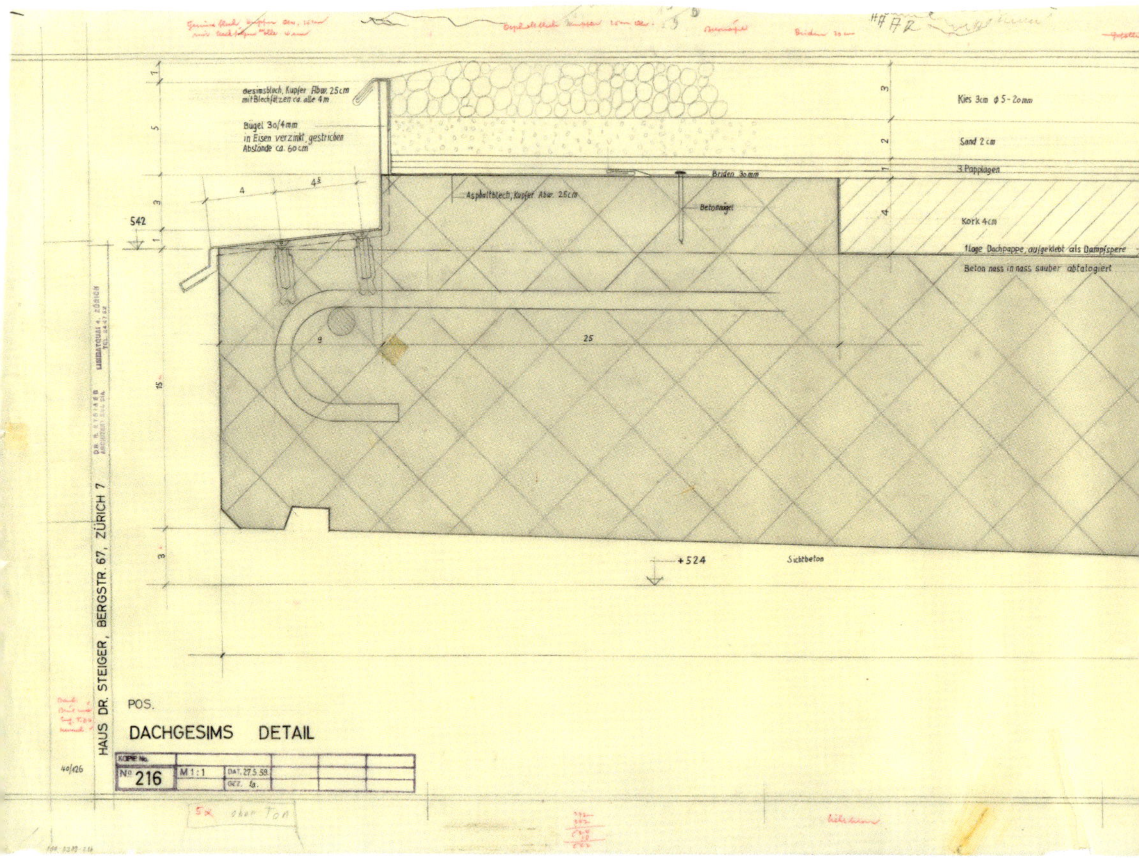

Roof detail, section

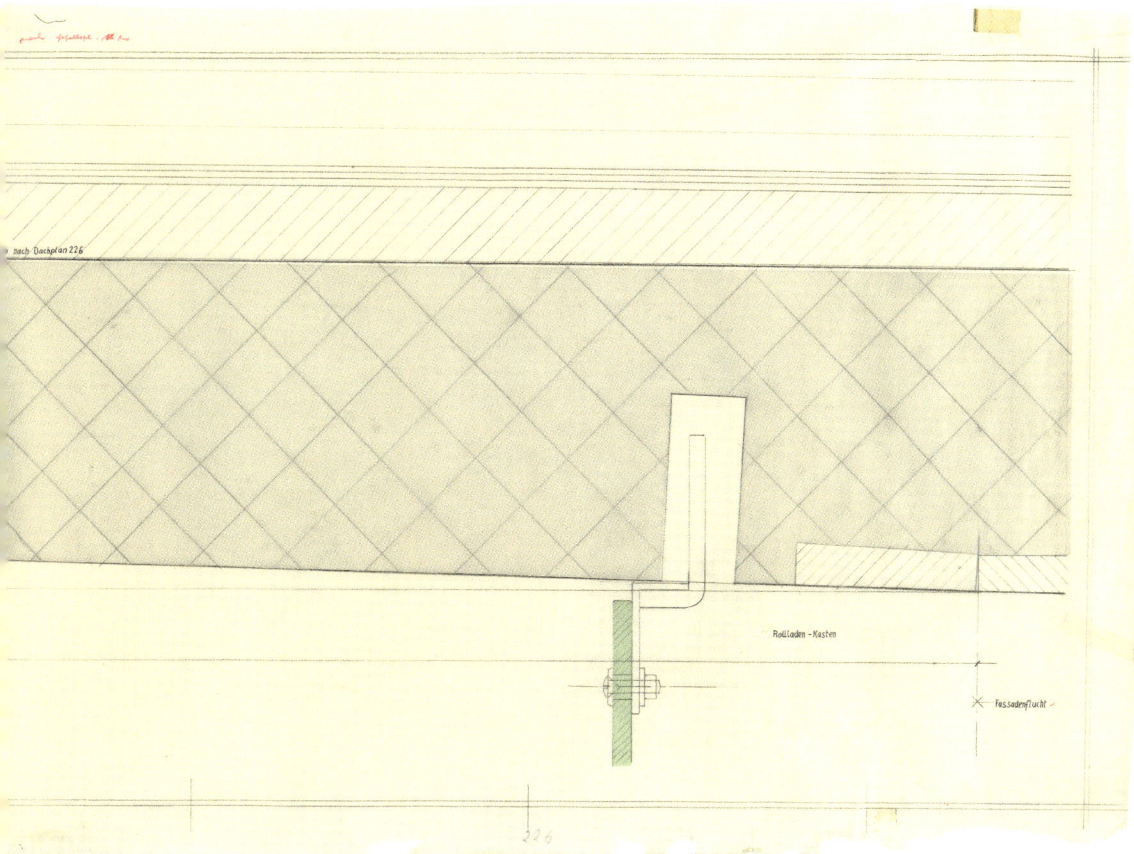
nach Dachplan 226
Rolladen-Kasten
Fassadenflucht
226

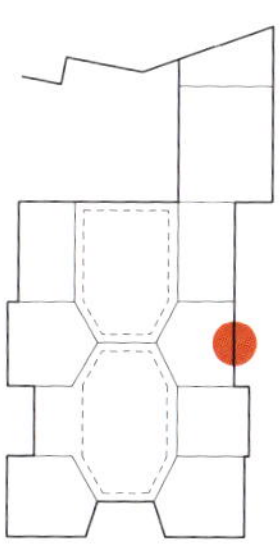

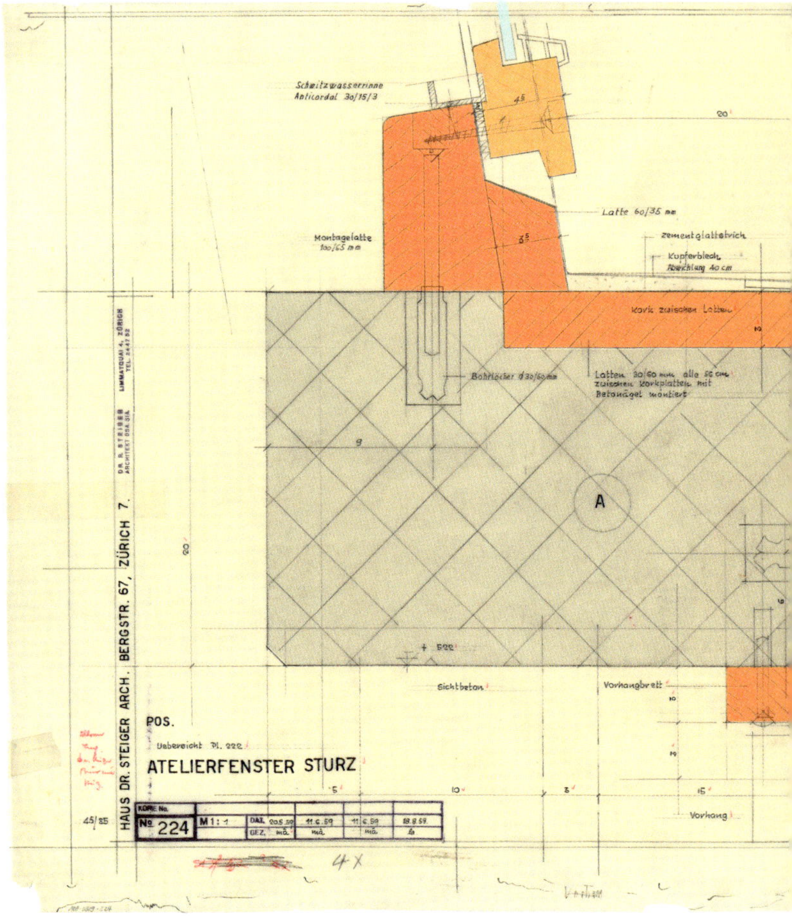

Garden door and window lintel, section

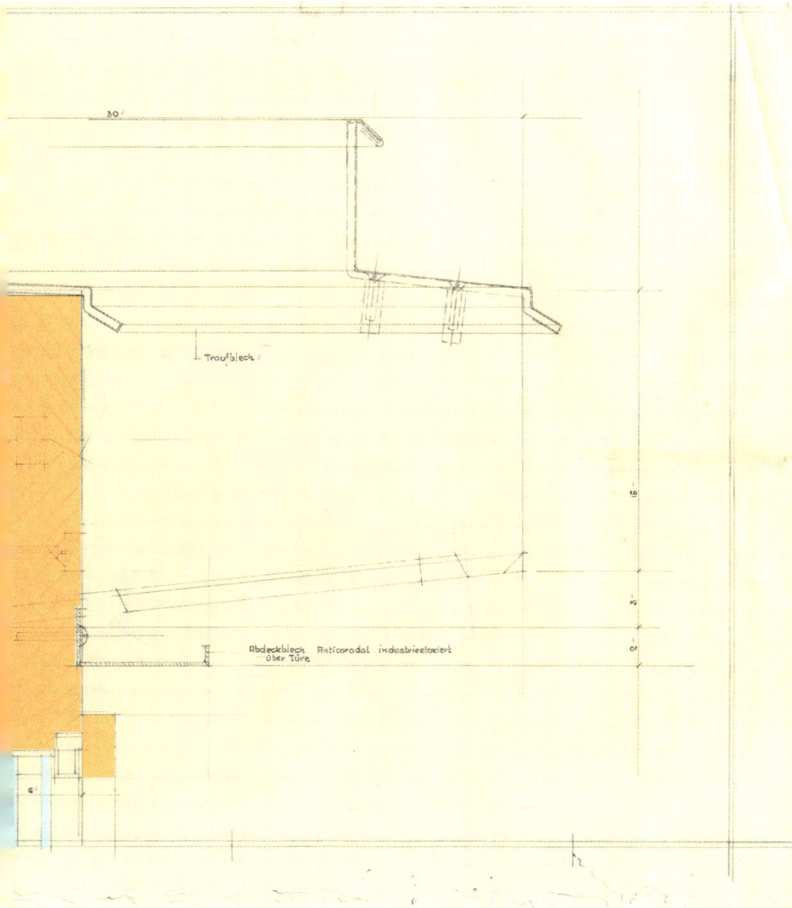
30
Traufblech
Abdeckblech Anticorodal industrieeloxiert
über Türe

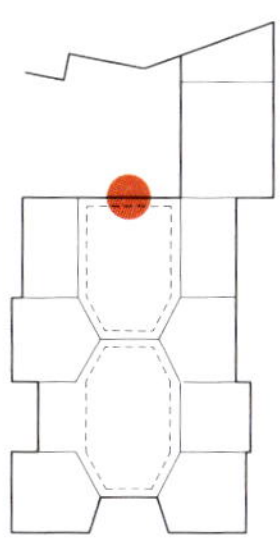

Facades

Moderate Modernism

The Steiger House is an example of moderate modernism,[40] which contrasts with heroic modernism: vertical windows, classic skylights rather than ribbon windows, a typical emphasis on corners, local symmetries, elements arranged additively as a concatenation, et cetera. The architects refer to elements of the imposing oeuvre by Haefeli Moser Steiger, in addition to the University Hospital Zurich (1938–1953), for example the Dental Institute (1954–1961): framing, infills, horizontality, striking eaves (University Hospital). The monumental pillars in the entrance hall reference the sculptural design used for the pillar of the ramp in the commercial building "Zur Palme" (1955–1964, built from 1959), constructed in the same period, and in terms of plasticity also cite the corner pillars of the "Bally-Capitol" commercial building (1961–1968, built from 1966).

The overall appearance of the facades[41] reflects the various portions of the floor plan: the glazed corner rooms, the recessed loggias, the staircase, and the utility wing. Local symmetries structure the facades. The two corner rooms and the "conical" inset loggia in the middle focus attention on a "large-scale" symmetry on the southeast side, while the window facades of the corner rooms with the two sliding windows and the small ventilation sashes on the sides display a "local" symmetry. The box-like framed window facade protrudes from the concrete wall, looking as if it is set in front of it as a non-load-bearing element. The studio's rear northwest-facing facade, the studio, and the set-back utility section with its high-set ribbon windows, vertical windows, and doors on the northeast side are also symmetrical. On the southwest side, the main facade repeats on the upper floor, reflecting the interior structure.

40 For the general overview of the work, see the basic publication *Haefeli Moser Steiger. Die Architekten der Schweizer Moderne*, eds. Sonja Hildebrand, Bruno Maurer and Werner Oechslin, exhib. cat., Museum für Gestaltung Zurich, Zurich, gta Verlag, 2007. In addition see also *O. R. Salvisberg. Die andere Moderne*, gta Verlag, 1985. The term was proposed by Martin Steinmann and Claude Lichtenstein. In contrast to the finely structured moderate modernism of the post-war period, this focused on the nineteen-twenties and nineteen-thirties, and in many cases is therefore more voluminous and monumental.

41 The 1970 addition is not part of the analysis.

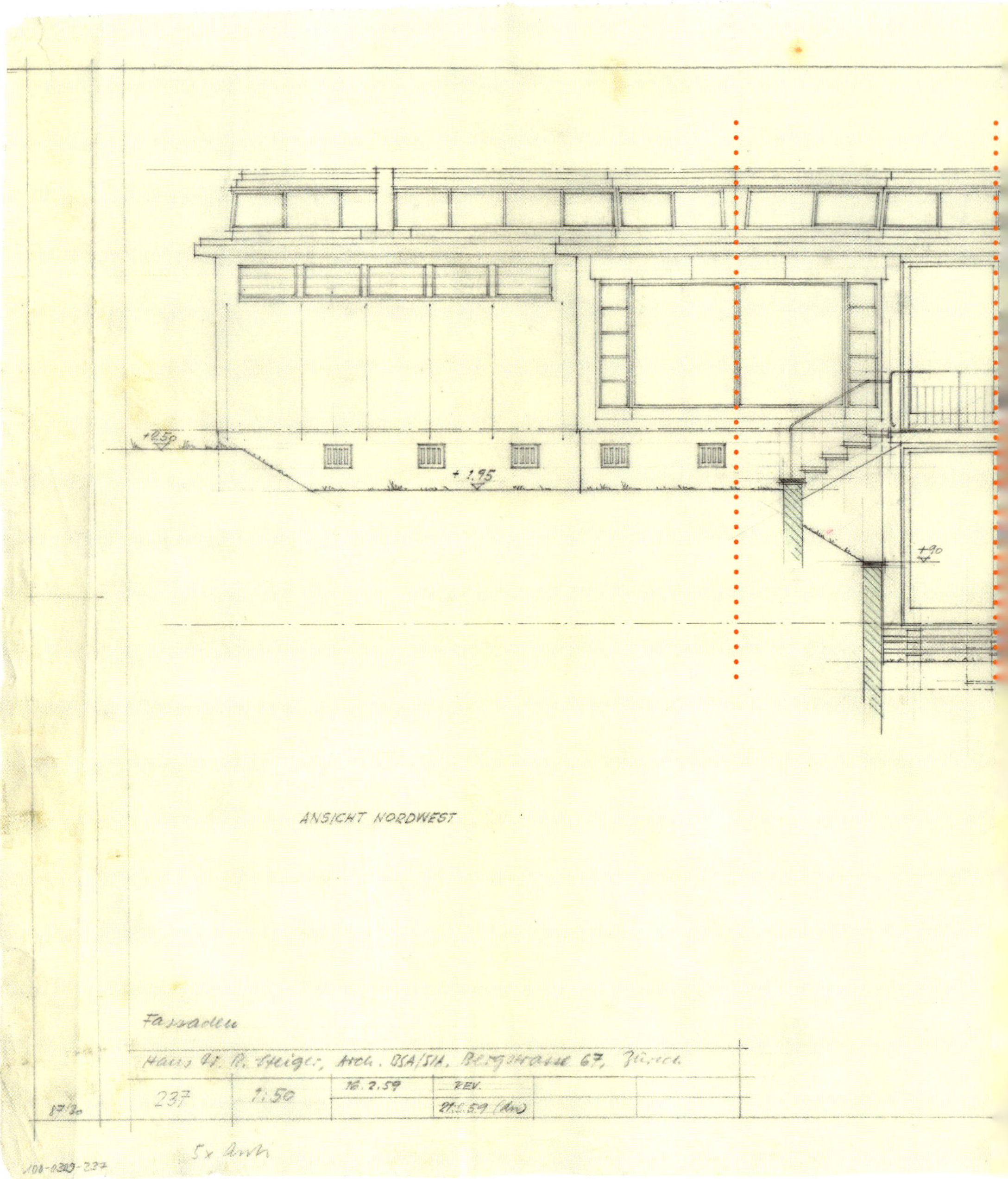

Southwest facade

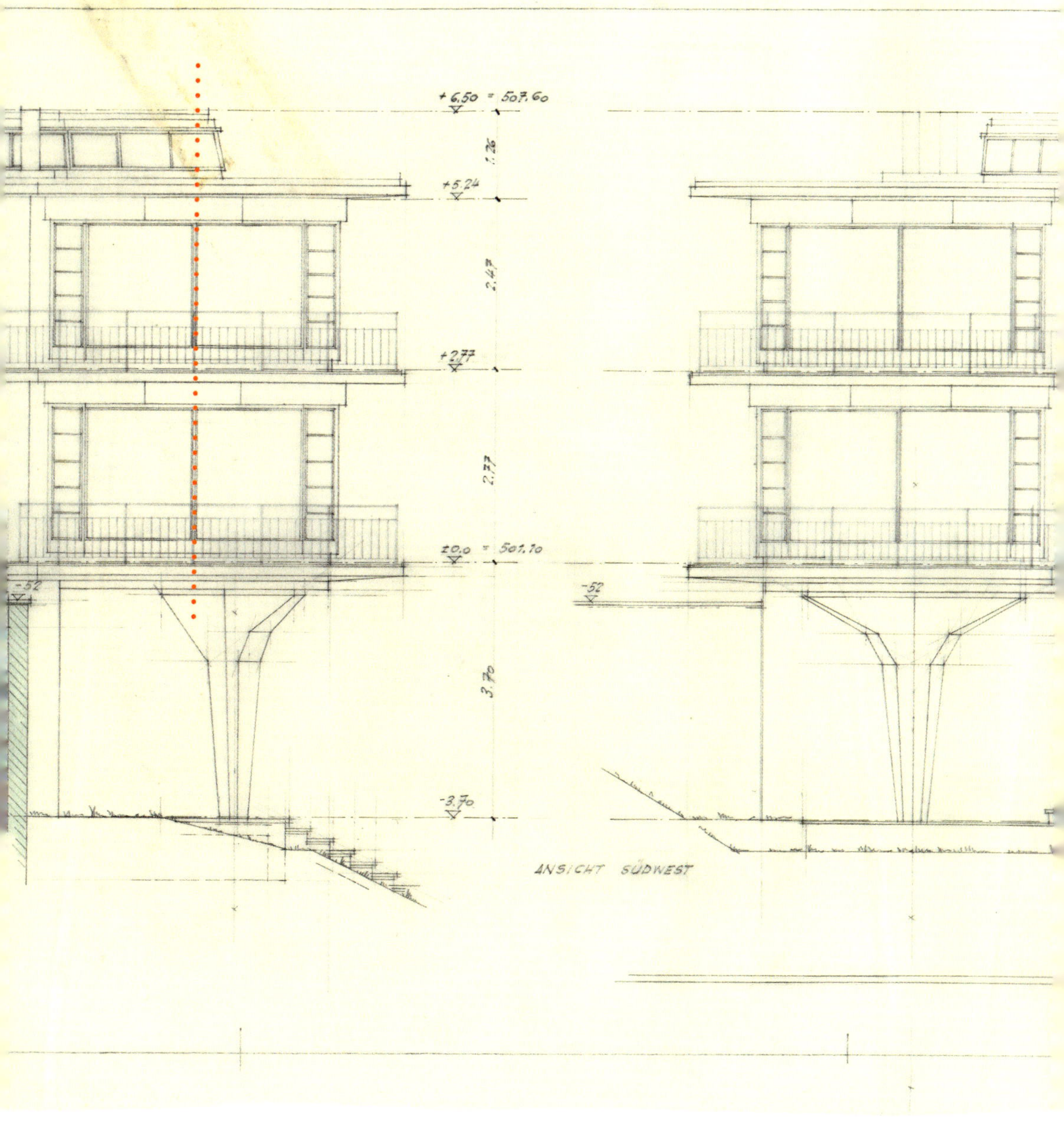

+6,50 = 507,60
1,26
+5,24
2,47
+2,77
2,77
±0,0 = 501,10
-52
3,70
-3,70
-52
ANSICHT SÜDWEST

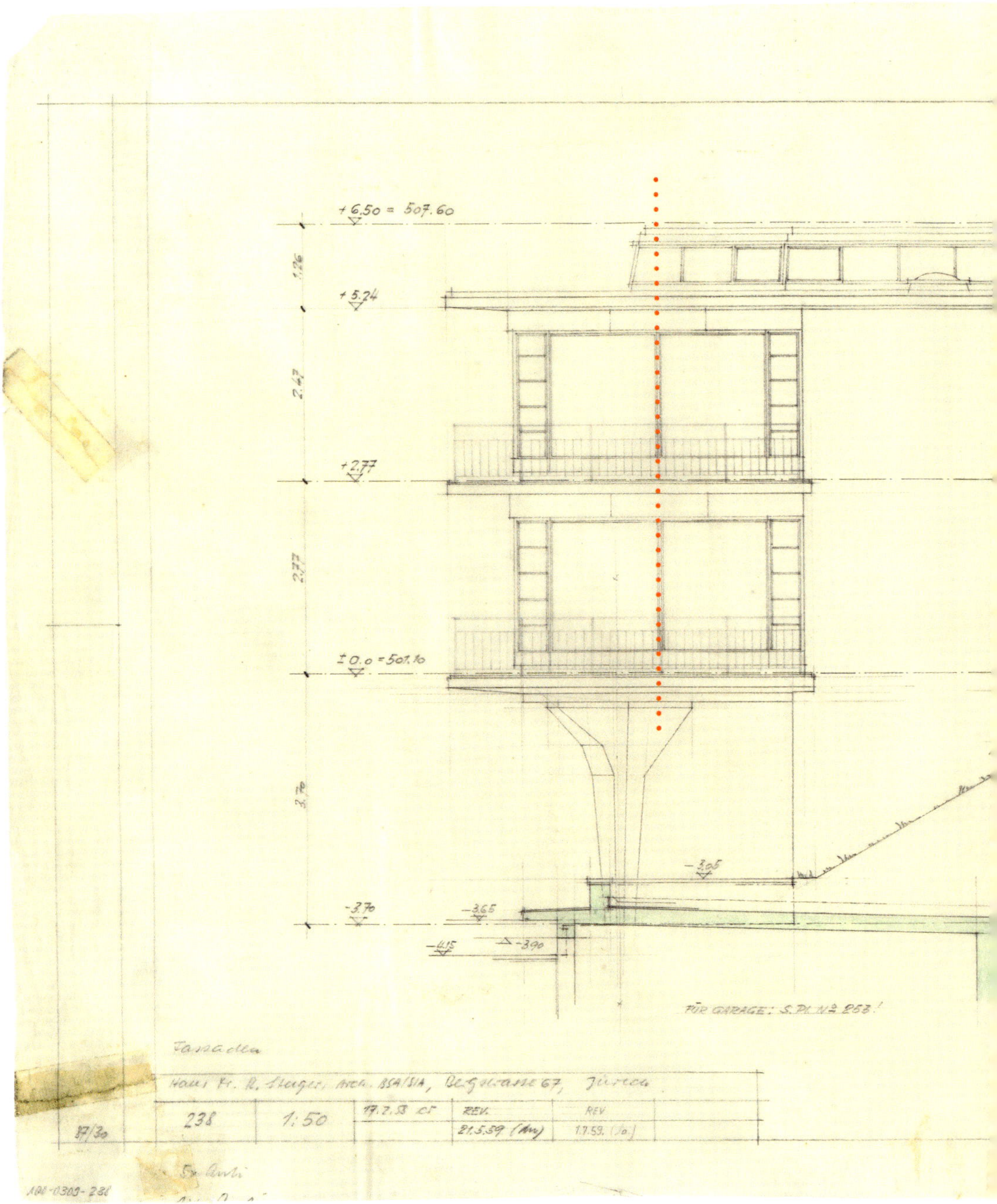

Northeast facade

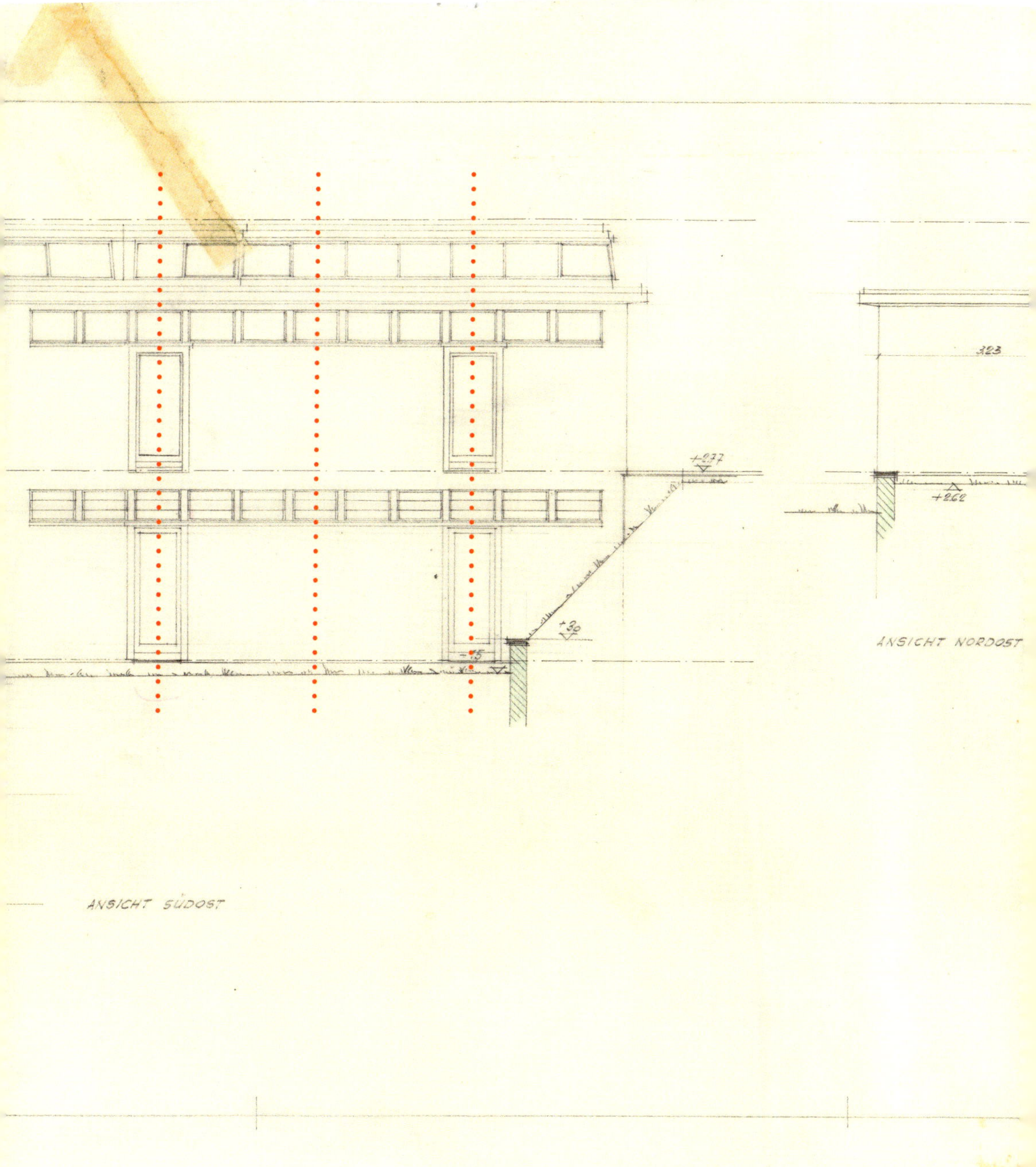

+2,77
+30
+2,62
3,23
ANSICHT SÜDOST
ANSICHT NORDOST

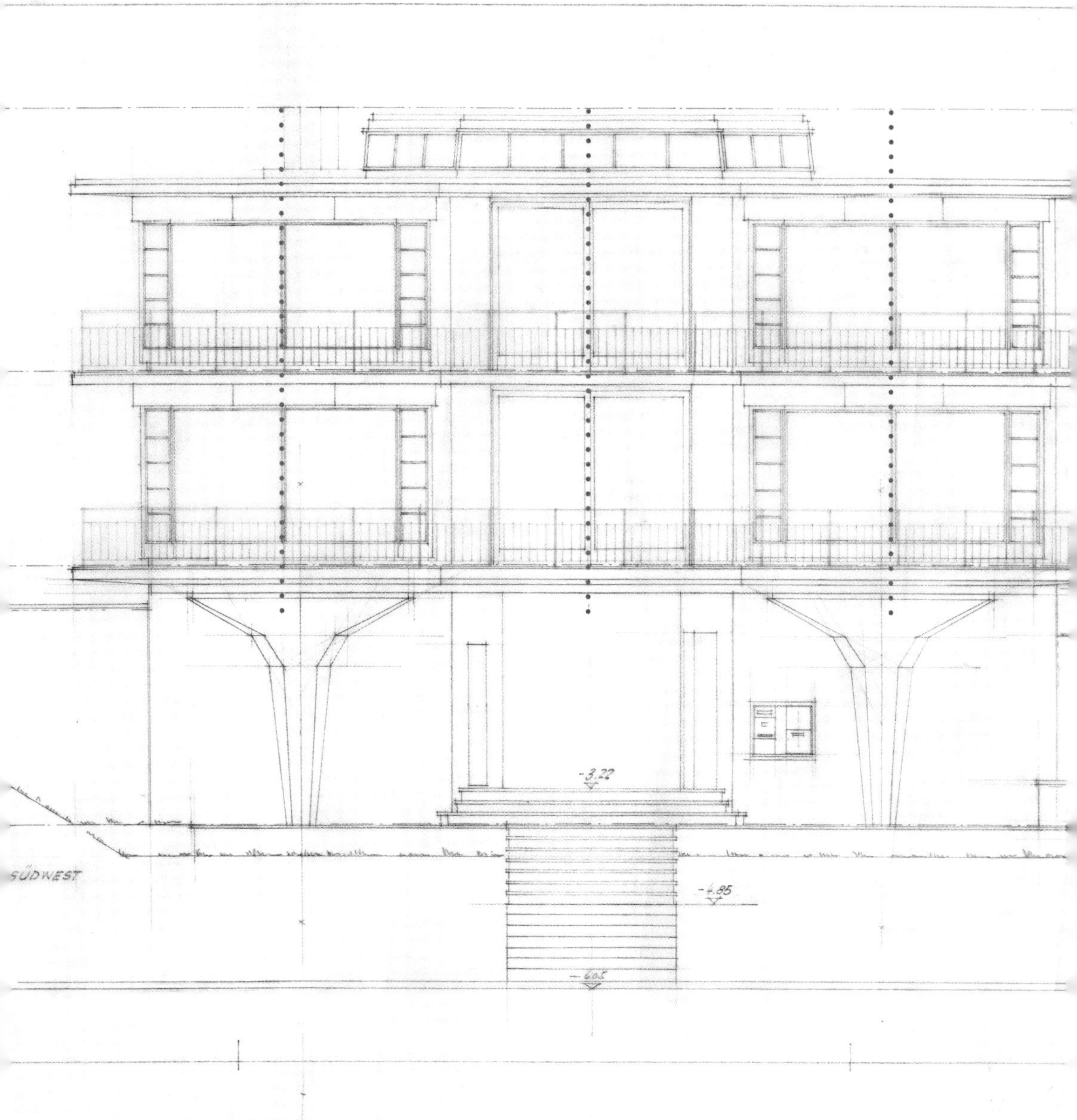

Southeast facade

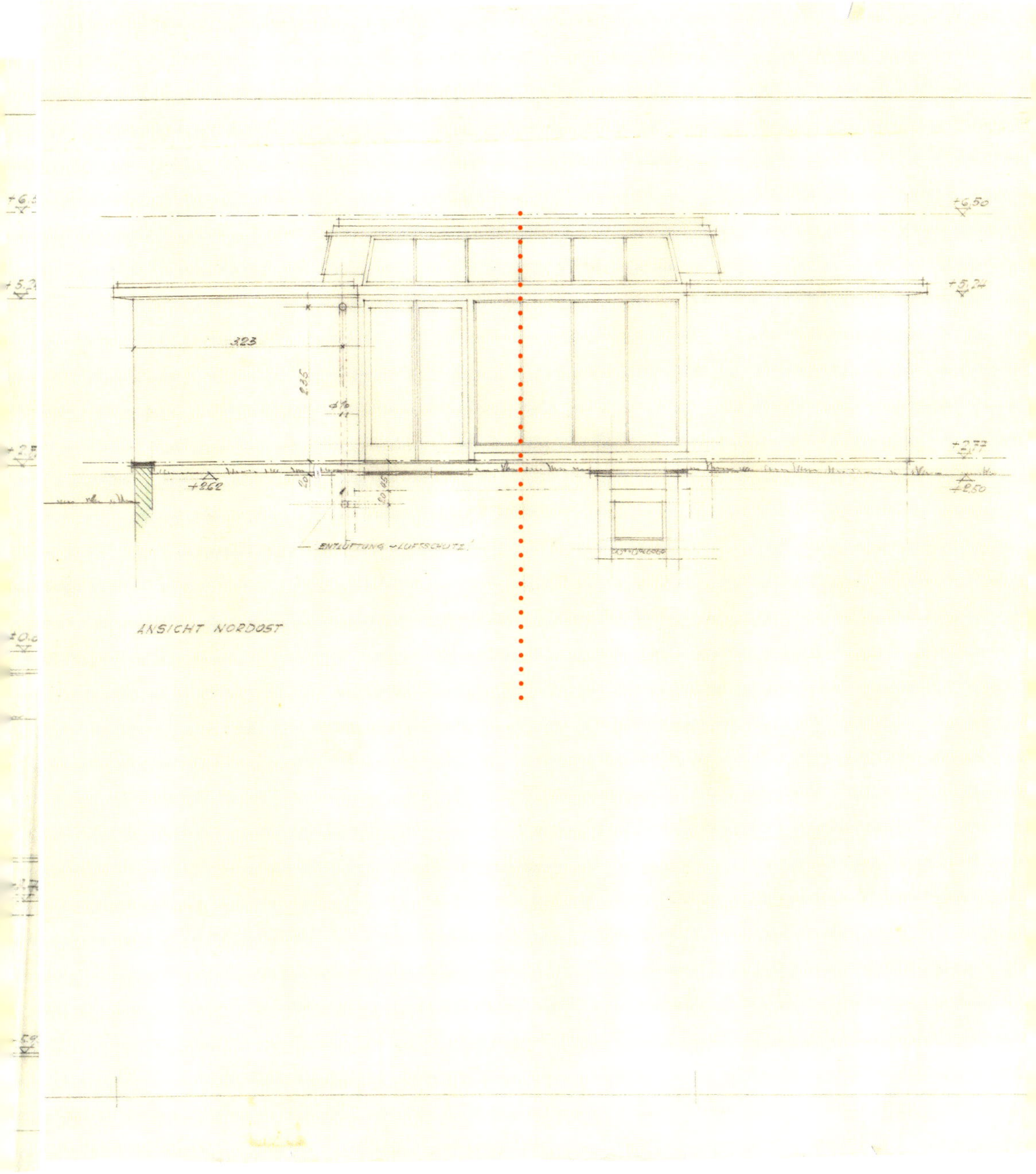

Northwest facade

Mechanization Takes Command

The process of mechanization taking command of the household, as described along with its historical background by Siegfried Giedion in his eponymous book,[42] occurred at the Steiger House in a sedate, discreetly traditional manner. The cable winches – old-school construction-site equipment – are one example. In addition to the small goods elevator, a cable winch was also incorporated into the main facade, attached to the cantilevered roof. Another such winch is located on the studio ceiling, above the opening to the sculpture cellar, which evokes an underground dungeon.

Small Goods Elevator and Milk Crate Niche – The Power of Tradition

A small goods elevator with a cable winch connects the first story and the upper level. A crate-sized niche for milk deliveries is positioned alongside it. Both were traditional elements of everyday life in nineteen-fities Switzerland: the administration-style goods elevator, hinting at efficiency, and the milk crates, always painted white for hygiene reasons, used by local farmers who still brought fresh milk to the city in person every day. The Plexiglas mailbox integrated into the front door next to the goods elevator can be operated from the inside.

Milk crate niche and mailbox

Small goods elevator

42 — Cf. Siegfried Giedion, *Mechanization Takes Command. A Contribution to Anonymous History*, New York, Oxford Press University, 1948. German edition with a comment by Stanislaus von Moos: *Die Herrschaft der Mechanisierung. Ein Beitrag zur anonymen Geschichte*, Frankfurt am Main, 1982.

Fittings

Many of the fittings may have been specially developed for the house. In the stairwell, a round bar connects the handle to the high projected window; the closing mechanism of the single-glazed corner windows works in a similar way. Max Haefeli's specially designed door handles were used throughout.

Tilt window

Opening roller shutters

Movie Screen and Blackout Shutters – Socializing

A retractable built-in screen for showing films is incorporated into the upper apartment, between the central space and the studio. The surrounding skylights are fitted with folding horizontal shutters to darken the room, operated by a crank with an ingenious deflection mechanism. A similar device is used to open the skylights (for ventilation).

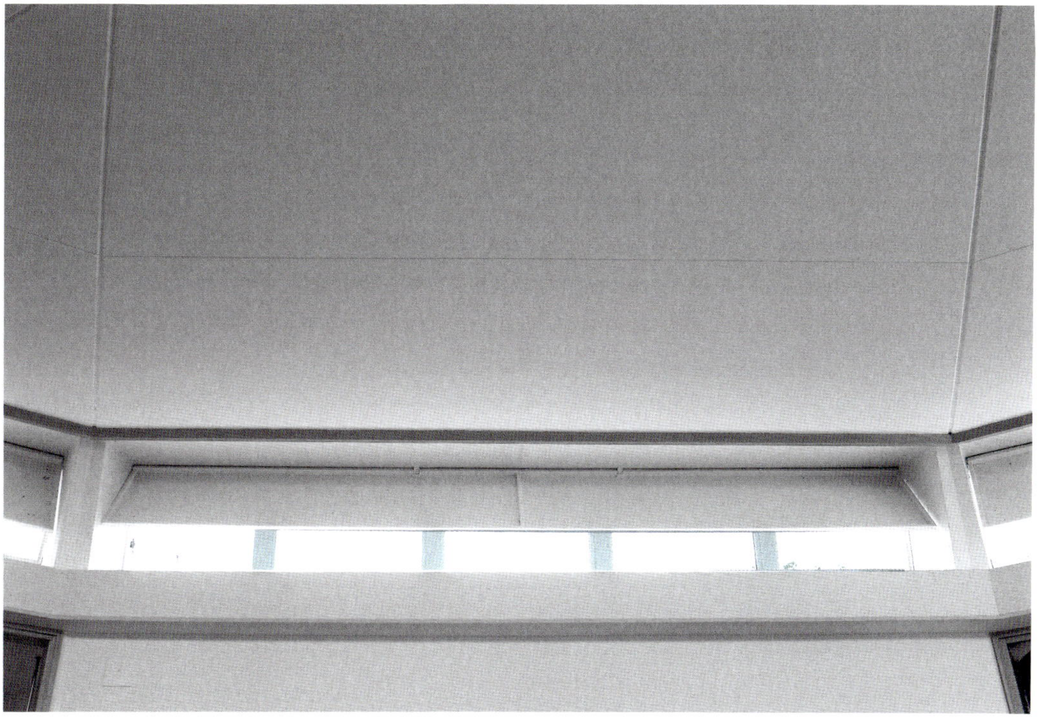

Street Lighting

Peter Steiger recounts that his parents' diary was crammed with cultural activities. Once a month, always on a Thursday, they held an open house evening, with friends and people from the world of culture coming and going. The street lighting, specially designed for the new access road, could be operated directly from the apartment, offering the option of welcoming guests out in the street or bidding them farewell there. The grand piano was certainly also used for intimate concerts in their home. Räto Tschupp, who founded the Camerata Zurich chamber orchestra (1957), lived in the lower apartment.

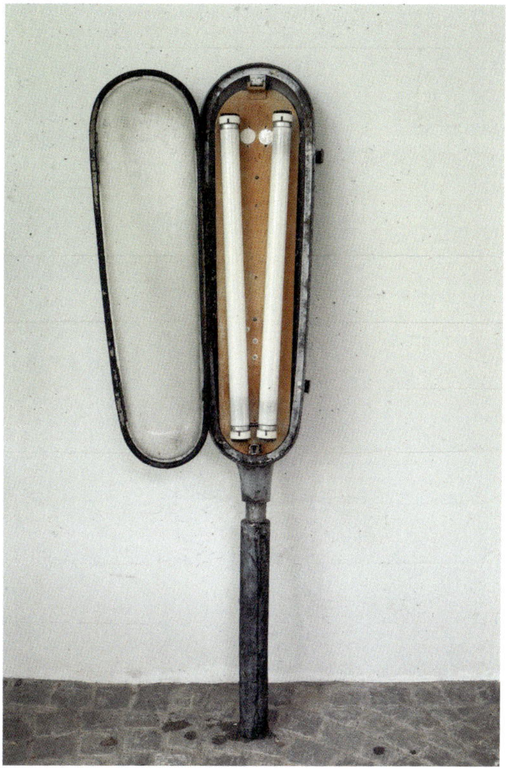
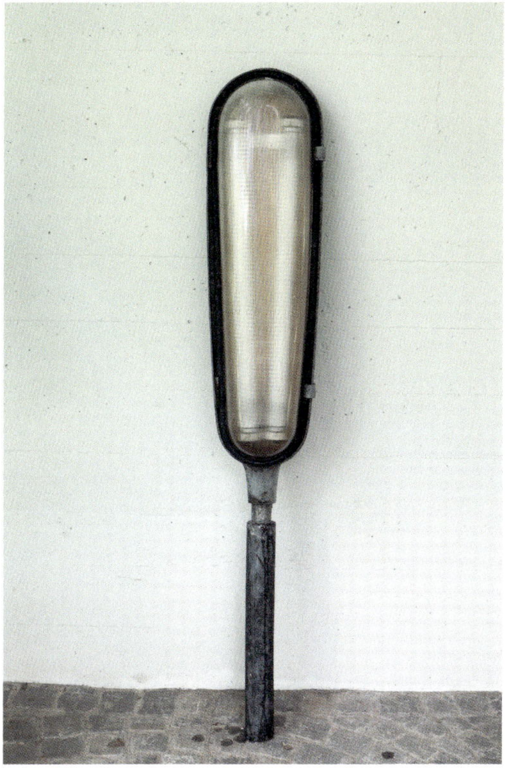

The Giedions together with the sculptor Étienne Hajdú (on the right).

The painting *La fleur jaune* (1944) by Fernand Léger, highly esteemed by Sigfried Giedion, was granted the place of honor in the room. Photo: Dolf Hüppi, circa 1960

Living with Art

Residing in Doldertal

Artful Living is the title of a trend-setting magazine. However, if New York creative director Felix Burrichter is to be believed, the term also refers to one of the probable models for future lifestyles – "a symphonic utopia where life imitates art."[43] That signifies a disciplined, luxurious form of existence that presupposes being surrounded by art, thus generating a "curated enchantment, a gesamt work of art."[44] Irrespective of how elite interior design may look in future, the alliance between art and life is probably as old as art. "Art per se wants to live," Markus Brüderlin comments, and "to take on new functions that are closer to everyday life by settling into a cozy home."[45] Although classical modernism – at least officially – abandoned the traditional "total work of art," it also experimented with a highly diverse range of ways to live with art. In Paris, for example, bourgeois bohemians rapidly appropriated the two-story artist's studio and transformed it from a creative space into a consumerist space, within which they celebrated a particularly intimate intermingling of avant-garde art, design, and a refined lifestyle with the help of key figures in the decorative arts, such as Louis Süe, Pierre Chareau or Robert Mallet-Stevens. The Parisian workshop-cum-studio was also the inspiration underlying Le Corbusier's Maison Citrohan – a box-shaped prototype house that he displayed in one of its countless variants at the Paris arts and crafts exhibition in 1925 to advocate a radical alternative to Art Deco's approach to designing space.

In German-speaking Switzerland, the great art collectors of the time preferred to complement their upper-class country houses with top-lit picture galleries: the Browns at Villa Langmatt (Baden, architect Karl Moser, 1904–1906) or the Hahnlosers at Villa Flora (Winterthur, architects Rittmeyer and Furrer, 1925). Contrasting with those extensive complexes, the "small open-air museum of modern architecture,"[46] that runs for around 200 meters along both sides of the Wolfbachtobel in Zurich-Hottingen, offered scope for more intimate transactions between art and living space. Within a very small area,

A Villa Giedion
Bischoff and Weideli

B Haefeli House
Max Haefeli

C Doldertal Houses
Marcel Breuer
Alfred and Emil Roth

D Steiger House
Rudolf Steiger
Flora Steiger-Crawford

E Fellowship Home
Alfred Roth

F Liesch House
Andres Liesch

eminent art historians, architects and artists built homes for themselves and their families there between 1924 and 1973. Despite the huge divergences in their aspirations and architectural views, they all felt the urge to give tangible expression to their affinity with art. Conceived as an experimental testing ground for "settling down within art," the seven buildings present astonishing insights into the "cozy home" of the art-loving Swiss intelligentsia in the first half of the twentieth century. From an international perspective, this architecture may be better integrated into everyday realities than glamorous Parisian salons, yet it nonetheless testifies to a comparably ambitious aspiration to define how lifestyle, architecture, and "high" art should interact.

Modernity, Autobiography, Art

In 1922, when successful Zurich architect Max Haefeli decided to build a home for his family in the uppermost, highly terraced section of the Doldertal

43 Felix Burrichter, introductory text to the chapter "Artful Living," in *This Will Be the Place. Thoughts and Photographs About the Future of Interiors*, ed. id, Milan et al., 2017, p. 139.

44 ibid.

45 Markus Brüderlin, "Einführung Interieur Exterieur. Die moderne Seele und ihre Suche nach der idealen Behausung," in *Interieur Exterieur. Wohnen in der Kunst. Vom Interieurbild der Romantik zum Wohndesign der Zukunft*, eds. id. and Annelie Lütgens, exhib. cat., Kunstmuseum Wolfsburg, Ostfildern, 2008, pp. 12–33, here p. 27.

46 Andres Giedion, "Im Doldertal," in Rüegg, 1996, pp 11–13, here p. 12.

(the left flank of the Wolfbachtobel), Villa Giedion, located in the lowest part of the valley, was barely six years old. The two buildings adopted the same room layout – at least on the first floor: vestibule, hallway, living room, dining room, veranda, kitchen – a room for every residential function, as was customary in bourgeois circles of the day (Haefeli included a master bedroom too). The similarities however stop there. Haefeli's modern "country house," inspired by role models in England and Germany, conveyed a clear break with the classicism of the "villa" that architects Bischoff and Weideli had built without any client commission in 1915/16 and sold to Bertha Giedion in 1917. Haefeli's approach chimed entirely with Peter Meyer's views as a pugnacious advocate of a modern lifestyle integrated into tradition: "In contrast to classical and neoclassical architecture, which focused entirely on prestige, ceremonial dignity, and symmetry, modern architecture aims to serve contemporary, bourgeois private life as modestly as possible, without grand gestures," and "directly, without interposing the 'formal language' it has developed between intention and form, as the classical formal language did."[47]

It comes as no surprise that Haefeli's "Doldertal House," completed in 1924, was the first entry in Meyer's compendium of modern Swiss residential buildings, the "gentle manifesto" of a rigorously cultivated modernity that was published by Hans Girsberger in 1928[48] – the annus mirabilis of modernist tubular steel furniture, as well as the year when the first of the International Congresses of Modern Architecture (Congrès Internationaux d'Architecture Moderne – CIAM) was held. The lowest common denominator in Meyer's examples – apart from the external appearance of the buildings, most with pitched roofs – is the "lively, organic cohesion of the rooms with one another."[49] Doors and stairways between the various levels interconnect the freely configured living spaces in Haefeli's design, as well as the terrace and veranda, creating an intriguing route through the house. Despite all the nuanced structuring of space, the restrained furnishings, which include Persian carpets and period furniture, often as stand-alone pieces, seem to function as a traditional means of signalling prestige. What about the art? It also fits as harmoniously as possible into the architecture. In the living room, fine pilaster strips determine the sequencing of the artworks, while in the entrance hall a magnificent Hodler adorns the radiator casing like an image of a saint on the altar.

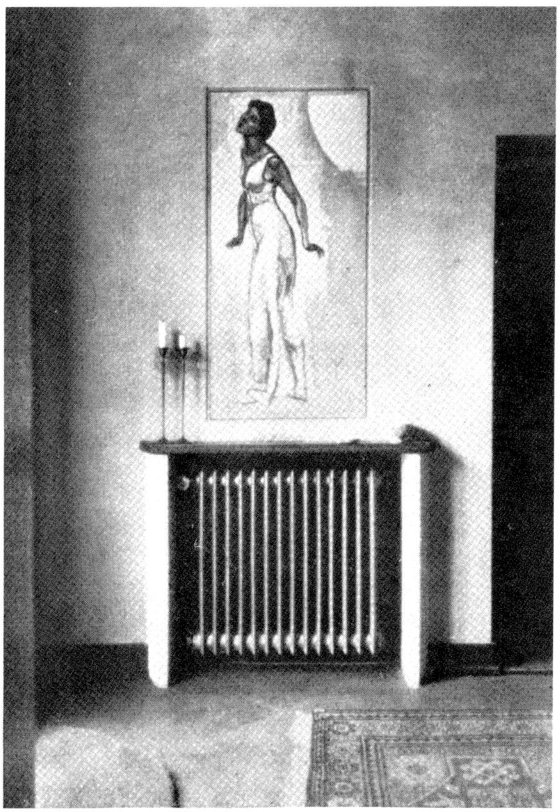

47 — Peter Meyer, *Moderne Schweizer Wohnhäuser*, Zurich, 1928, p. 13.

48 — Katharina Medici-Mall, *Im Durcheinandertal der Stile. Architektur und Kunst im Urteil von Peter Meyer (1894–1984)*, Basel et al., 1998, p. 160–170.

49 — Meyer 1928, p. 11; Meyer references the rural houses by Hermann Muthesius and – above all – by Theodor Fischer.

In contrast to the "vibrant, organic" layout of Haefeli's design, Villa Giedion's floor plan appears rigid, if not unimaginative. The living and dining rooms, extending a similar distance into the building and separately accessible from the hallway, are connected by a sliding door; the only reason why the veranda, arranged as an extension of the dining room, does not complete the symmetrical enfilade, is that it references the center of the main structure. This simple schematic plan, derived from the hôtel particulier and tried and tested a thousand times, once again proves its worth. However, art historians Sigfried Giedion and Carola Giedion-Welcker, who moved into the Giedion family villa in 1926, were not seduced by the *culte de l'axe* (cult of the axis). Their art collection little by little overran the relatively plain rooms, without reflecting any compositional considerations, in stark contrast to Haefeli's home. In 1926, Giedion's first major purchase was Carlo Carrà's *Solitudine* (Solitude) (1917); subsequently, he and his wife rapidly met virtually all the important avant-garde artists: "They were able to meet Constantin Brâncuși, to see Pablo Picasso's *Guernica* while it was in his studio, to help support the impoverished and embattled Piet Mondrian and to entertain Hans Arp on a regular basis."[50] Their magnificent art collection reflected their friendly interactions with the artists they admired and constituted, as Carola Giedion-Welcker noted, "our world in which one is happy."[51]

Their unconventional approach extended beyond the way in which the numerous masterpieces were hung. Late photographs show layers of books, paintings, photograms, graphic designs, newspaper clippings, bric-a-brac, and postcards covering the walls, alongside new tubular steel furniture, wing chairs and Baroque chests of drawers. By 1930, if not earlier, Giedion had encountered a similar conglomeration of objects in Le Corbusier's apartment at Rue Jacob 20, more evocative of a late medieval scholar's cabinet of curiosities than the nerve center for a prophet proclaiming the architecture of the future. Le Corbusier and the Giedions seem to have been fascinated by precisely that initially perplexing juxtaposition of visual references, accorded equal status and displayed in parallel – somewhat reminiscent of vilified nineteenth-century bourgeois tastes.[52] Both apartments were above all places for autobiographical reflection: homes in which ideas and programs could be simultaneously presented and recalled.

Housing as a Cultural Policy Program

However, Giedion by no means retreated into the academic ivory tower, on the contrary. From his Doldertal 7 headquarters he led a program as CIAM's influential Secretary-General that comprised a series of local operations, all tied into practical struggles to foster modern architecture. His contributions included promoting a politically and socially committed magazine (*information*, 1932/33), collaborating with Kunsthaus Zurich, supporting Zurich Werkbund and CIAM architects, and actively marketing a new lifestyle with the help of the furnishings firm he co-founded, Wohnbedarf AG, as well as constructing two model apartment blocks in the orchard at his home.

The story of how the "Doldertal houses" came into being has been recounted elsewhere.[53] Apparently, the Giedions initially considered selling their villa through a real estate agent to help fund the project.[54] It comes as no surprise that they opted not to move into one of the villa-like apartments built by Alfred and Emil Roth along with Marcel Breuer in 1935/36,[55] for the rooms have relatively modest dimensions, although the architects managed "to provide a balanced solution to the unusual demands of the site on the edge of the Doldertal gorge and fulfil the postulate of 'Befreites Wohnen' ('liberated dwelling') which the client, Sigfried Giedion, had reduced to the formula of 'light, air and openness as early as 1929. This was done with unrepeatable precision and with the aid of the most up-to-date structural and sanitary techniques."[56] Deft interlocking of interior and exterior space creates a sense of generous proportions, for example by establishing a diagonal visual relationship across the terrace to the side of the living room or breaking down the spatial boundary in the bay window-like porch with its exposed supports. However, this demonstratively modern

50 Cf. *Modern Masters. Works from a Private Swiss Collection*, auct. cat. Christie's London, London, 2014, p. 7.

51 Carola Giedion-Welcker, letter to Marcel Breuer, October 17th, 1934, quoted in Iris Bruderer-Oswald, *Das neue Sehen. Carola Giedion-Welcker und die Sprache der Moderne*, Bern et al, 2007, p. 104. The passage refers to the exhibition at Kunsthaus Zurich that Sigfried Giedion helped to organize: *Abstrakte Malerei und Plastik* (Abstract Painting and Sculpture) (10/11–11/4/1934).

52 Cf. on this point Arthur Rüegg, "Autobiographische Interieurs. Die Wohnungen Le Corbusiers," in *Le Corbusier. The Art of Architecture*, eds. Alexander von Vegesack et al., Vitra Design Museum, Weil am Rhein, 2007, pp. 117–161, here p. 129.

53 Cf. Rüegg 1996.

54 A. Graf, Immobilienagentur, Zurich 1, letter to Sigfried Giedion, November 16th, 1933, gta Archiv, ETH Zurich.

55 Alfred Roth put it in the following terms: "to transfer the advantages of the single-family home to the apartment." (Alfred Roth, "Zwei Mehrfamilienhäuser im Doldertal," in *Werk*, 23, 9, 1936, pp. 285–290, here p. 289.)

56 Stanislaus von Moos, "Alfred Roth und die 'Neue Architektur'," in *Alfred Roth, Architect of Continuity / Architekt der Kontinuität*, Zurich, 1985, pp. 9–33, here p. 20.

receptacle was ill-adapted to the lifestyle adopted by this art-historian couple and to their overflowing flood of documents.

Shortly after the building was completed in spring 1936, however, Giedion had an architecture exhibition set up in Doldertal 17 that did not accommodate even the slightest gesture acknowledging the past. Alfred Roth had already prepared drawings the year before, portraying the prototype for the interior design with the latest furniture by Marcel Breuer and Alvar Aalto, as well as adding the serving trolley Roth had designed to the ensemble at the last minute. Precisely placed, Roth's *Komposition in Rot, Blau, Gelb* (Composition in Red, Blue and Yellow) by Piet Mondrian and Giedion's wooden relief *Objets placés sous les lois du hasard* (Objects Placed According to the Laws of Chance) by Hans Arp underscored the emphatically international nature of the designs. Thanks to Hans Finsler's masterful photographs, this didactic formulation of "liberated dwelling" had an immense impact. The eclectic group of tenants in the four main apartments actually had no particular aptitude for art and furnishings.[57] Giedion was forced to "sell off" his apartments during this crisis-plagued period; only Alfred Roth continued to demonstrate in one of the attic studios how the experiment had been intended.

Roth later viewed his residences as societal centers in which he could communicate his architectural and artistic stance. In 1960/61, a few years after his appointment to ETH Zurich, he put his ideal concept of a living and working space into practice on the opposite side of the Wolfbachtobel in the form of a studio house in which he could exchange ideas with like-minded people.[58] The elongated Fellowship Home – the name pays tribute to Frank Lloyd Wright's Taliesin Fellowship, while the shape is vaguely reminiscent of Le Corbusier's Citrohan House, which Roth was in charge of building in Stuttgart in 1927 – is an architectural hybrid: Roth's architecture and painting studio in the basement, five student rooms with a kitchen and dining area on the upper floor, and at the top a twenty-meter-long sequence of rooms for the architect, punctuated solely by two cubic volumes. Roth ran an open house here. Surrounded by Aalto furniture, he demonstrated what Charlotte Perriand – an old acquaintance from his Parisian days – described as "l'art d'habiter" ("the art of living"), more or less in full public view. He presented his artworks hung as if in a gallery, some in side-lit niches along the zigzag-shaped west wall. Together with a few pieces by Roth himself, these included oil paintings by Mondrian,

Le Corbusier, Baumeister, Vordemberge-Gildewart, and a pastel by Van de Velde; during his legendary tea parties, these cherished memories of early encounters with "pioneers" of modernism,[59] served Roth as springboards for anecdotes highlighting his aesthetic and cultural convictions.

Two Types of Artists' Houses

His immediate neighbor pursued her artistic inclinations even more vigorously: Flora Steiger-Crawford, four years older than Roth, had given up her original career in 1938 to become a professional sculptor. She had lived and worked with her husband, Rudolf, for a long time in sometimes precarious or at least cramped conditions. It therefore comes as no surprise that in 1958 the couple deliberately defied the steep topography to fulfil a long-standing dream in their own home "in the Wolfbachtöbeli"[60] and implemented a carefully honed ideal combination of living and working areas. A spacious, slightly elevated living room with a dining table and grand piano, set high on the slope between slim projecting slabs, is placed at the heart of an elongated centralized floor plan;[61] an equally large studio and smaller spaces are arranged around it, with the specific function of each determined by its position. Theoretically, ingenious sliding folding doors could have partitioned off the two small workspaces that look across the Dolder valley and the bedroom, which is laterally oriented along the slope, but these spaces seem to have been conceived as an integral part of the open-plan arrangement, like the fireplace alcove and the terrace, positioned along the axis of symmetry and oriented towards the Wolfbach stream. In contrast, the elongated sculptor's studio, elevated like the living room and lit by means of a strip of skylights, is largely closed off; the ceremonial mise-en-scène of the view of the hillside garden and Flora Steiger-Crawford's sculpted

57 — Cf. Giedion 1996, p. 12.

58 — Cf. von Moos 1985, pp. 29 f.

59 — Cf. Alfred Roth, *Begegnung mit Pionieren. Le Corbusier, Piet Mondrian, Adolf Loos, Josef Hoffmann, Auguste Perret, Henry van de Velde*, Basel et al., 1973.

60 — Flora Steiger-Crawford, autobiography, in *Flora Steiger-Crawford 1899–1991*, Zurich, 2003, pp. 24–98, here p. 92.

61 — Palladio's Villa Rotonda is generally cited as a source of inspiration. However, the floor plan is also as succinct as a simple "bubble diagram."

62 — Peter Steiger in conversation with the author on 11/25/2017.

figures, some larger than life, was apparently reserved for occasions when socializing was on the agenda.[62]

The furniture, interspersed with Flora Steiger-Crawford's own creations, is intriguing from a design-history perspective. The robust dining table was among the solid, modern basic furnishings that she had developed specifically for her retirement residence. It is combined with comparatively sleek *Neues Bauen* mass-produced *Typenmöbel* (functional furniture)[63] – such as the rare Steiger table with a tubular steel base, supplemented with a new wooden tabletop, the "Steiger wheeled storage units" and the occasional Haefeli chair – casually combined with anonymous colonial-style chairs, wicker furniture and upholstered armchairs. Numerous abstract, figurative sculptures by the artist herself and Rudolf Steiger's oil painting *Acropolis* add the finishing touches to the interior, every detail imbued with Steiger-Crawford's work and ideas. Unlike the non-representational collections put together by the Giedions or Alfred Roth, the rest of the art program was also permeated by a "new tradition" that underlined a sense of continuity, which Franz Müller associated with terms like "classicism," "realism," and "timelessness."[64] Max Gubler, Ernst Kissling, Louis Conne, Hans Fischli, and Walter Kurt Wiemken numbered among the artists in their circles whose works helped set the mood in the rooms.

Ten years later, Grisons-born architect Andres Liesch implemented an almost identical spatial program on the neighboring plot on the valley side, but in a completely different architectural idiom; rather than creating a lightweight tree house, this building is composed as a stepped structure that appears to have melded with the mountain. Liesch made the most of the steep slope, stacking up a duplex and a triplex apartment, above which he built a two-story studio house with a hexagonal floor plan for himself and artist Madlaina Demarmels.[65] In contrast to Rudolf and Flora Steiger's home, the dining alcove, the living room, and the two studios are lined up along the south facade, framed spatially by a freestyle composition of monolithic walls. Chiming with the shell limestone flooring and built-in smoked-oak furniture, the untreated exposed concrete gives the rooms a sculptural solidity that renders the numerous paintings and sculptures – including several by Ödön Koch – all the more radiant. Precisely positioned apertures and vistas, along with a sophisticated lighting control system, underscore the flow of space and give the dark walls a pleasantly warm, almost textile-like feel, depending on the incident light. Almost all the furnishings were fitted, with the exception of the dining-room ensemble, a seating area with two Corbusier sofas, and the pared-down work tables. Like Flora Steiger-Crawford, Madlaina Demarmels lived alone for a long time in this concrete castle, meticulously designed down to the last detail. In her final years, she worked on pointillist structures suggesting movement in her "Pittura moleculara" ("Molecular Painting") series, in which she carefully opened and deepened the solid architectural frame of the building.

Today, the artist Seraina Feuerstein lives and works in the Liesch House.

63 Cf. Arthur Rüegg, "Die Möbel," in *Flora Steiger-Crawford 2003*, pp. 140–151.

64 Cf. Franz Müller, "Die Plastikerin," in *Flora Steiger-Crawford 2003*, pp. 152–163.

65 Cf. Susanna Koeberle, "Zürich und Chur: Meisterbauten," in *Ideales Heim, 2, 2002*, pp. 34–45.

A Villa Giedion
Bischoff and Weideli
1916

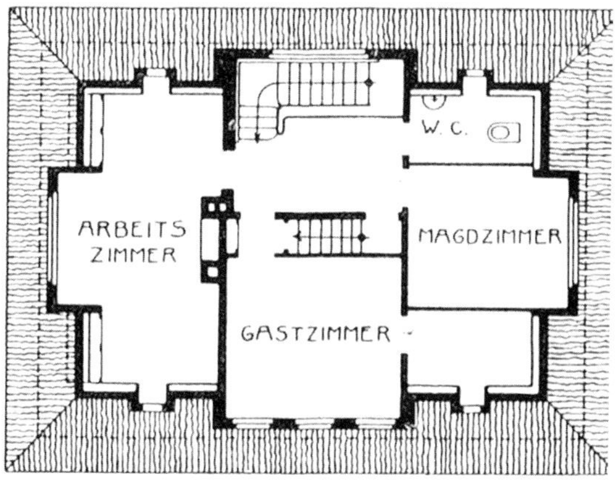
W.C.
ARBEITS ZIMMER
MAGDZIMMER
GASTZIMMER

1:200

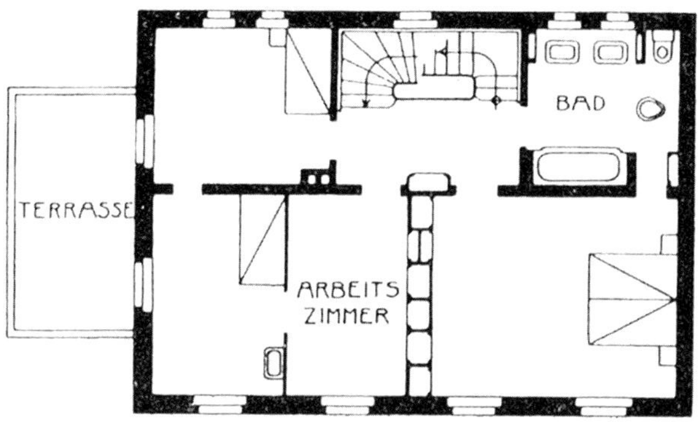
BAD
TERRASSE
ARBEITS ZIMMER

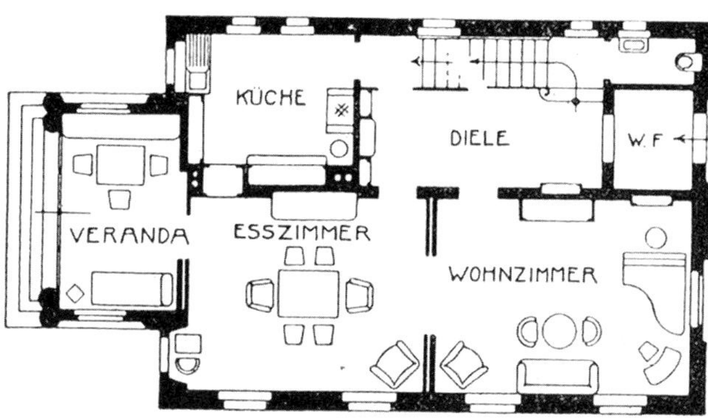
KÜCHE
DIELE
W.F
VERANDA
ESSZIMMER
WOHNZIMMER

B

Haefeli House

Max Haefeli

1924

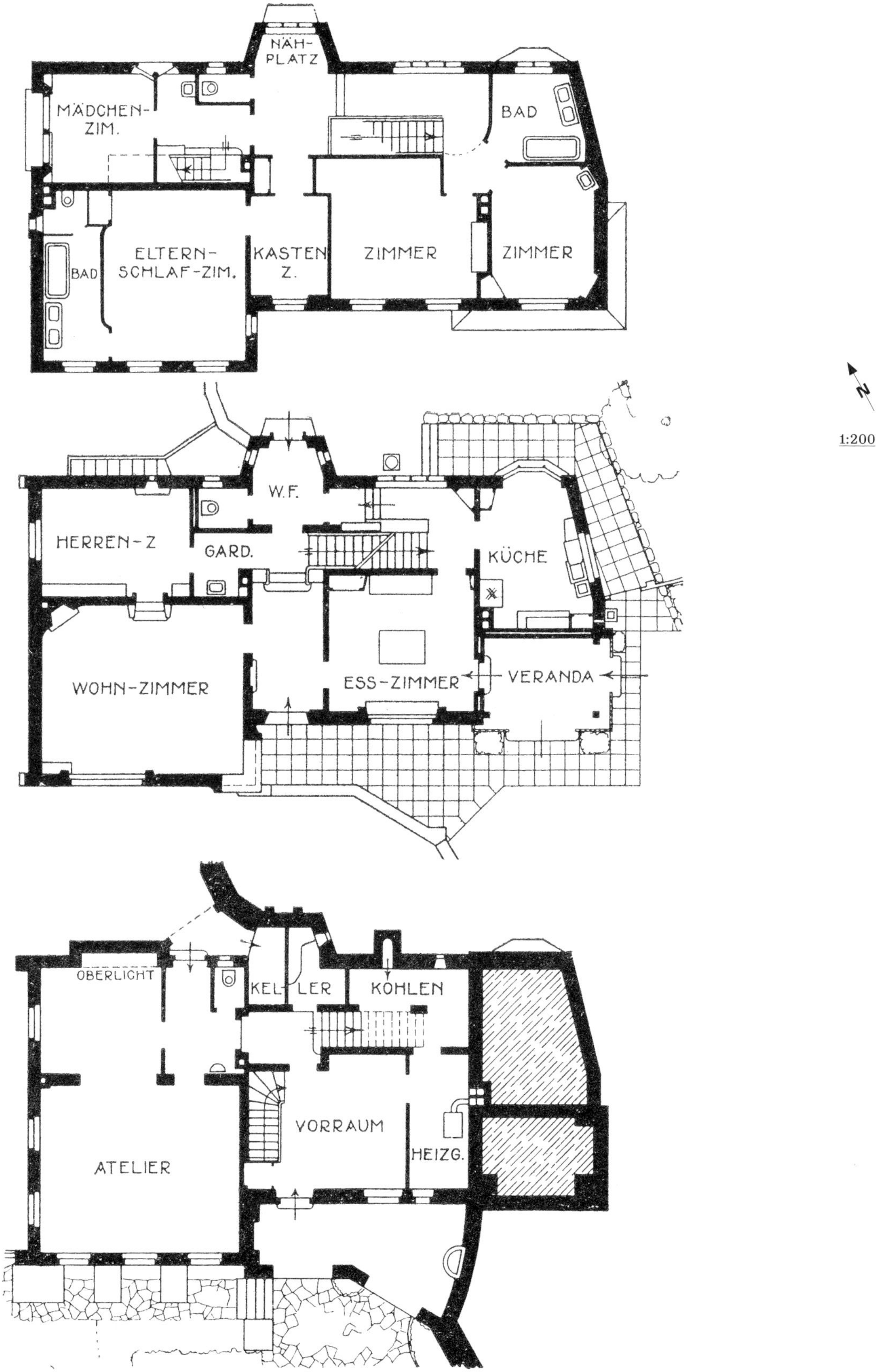
NÄH-
PLATZ
MÄDCHEN-
ZIM.
BAD
BAD
ELTERN-
SCHLAF-ZIM.
KASTEN
Z.
ZIMMER
ZIMMER
W.F.
HERREN-Z
GARD.
KÜCHE
WOHN-ZIMMER
ESS-ZIMMER
VERANDA
OBERLIGHT
KEL LER
KOHLEN
VORRAUM
HEIZG.
ATELIER
N
1:200

C

Doldertal Houses

Marcel Breuer

Alfred and Emil Roth

1936

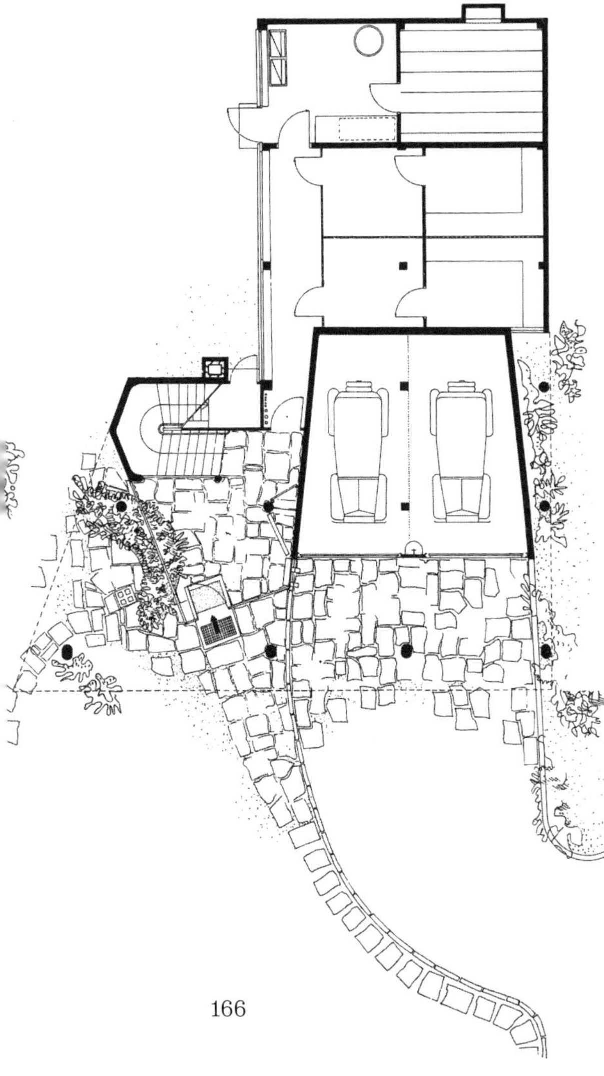

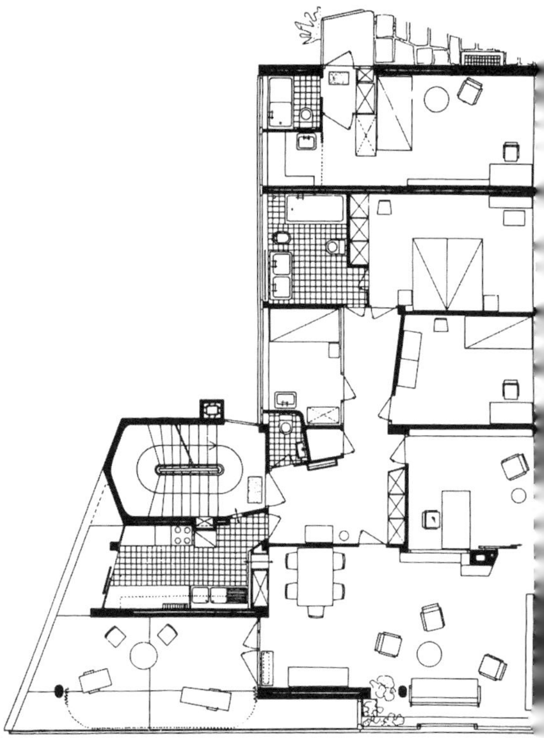

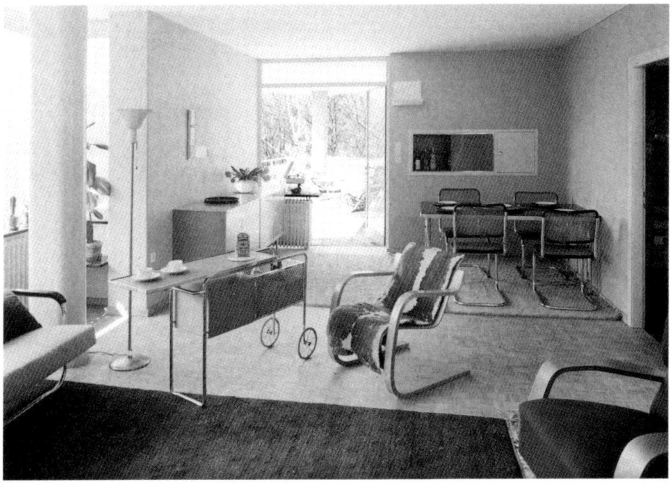

1:200

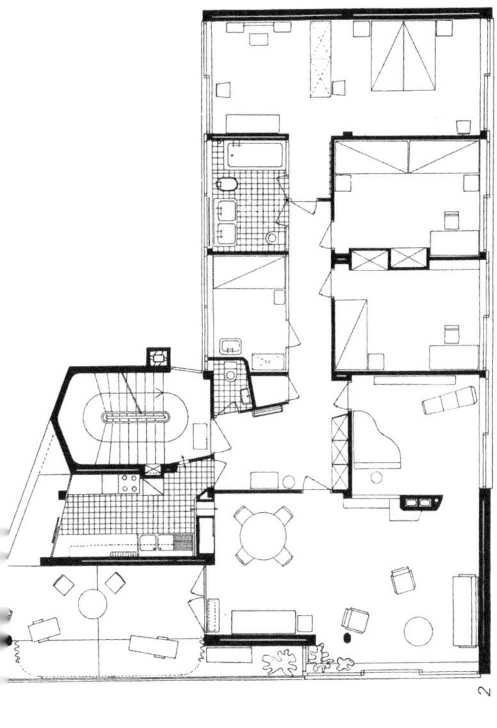

2

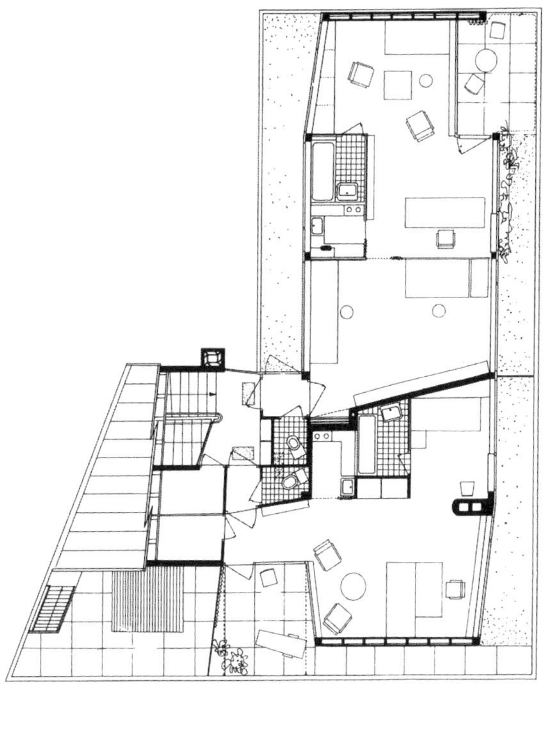

D Steiger House

Rudolf Steiger

Flora Steiger-Crawford

1959

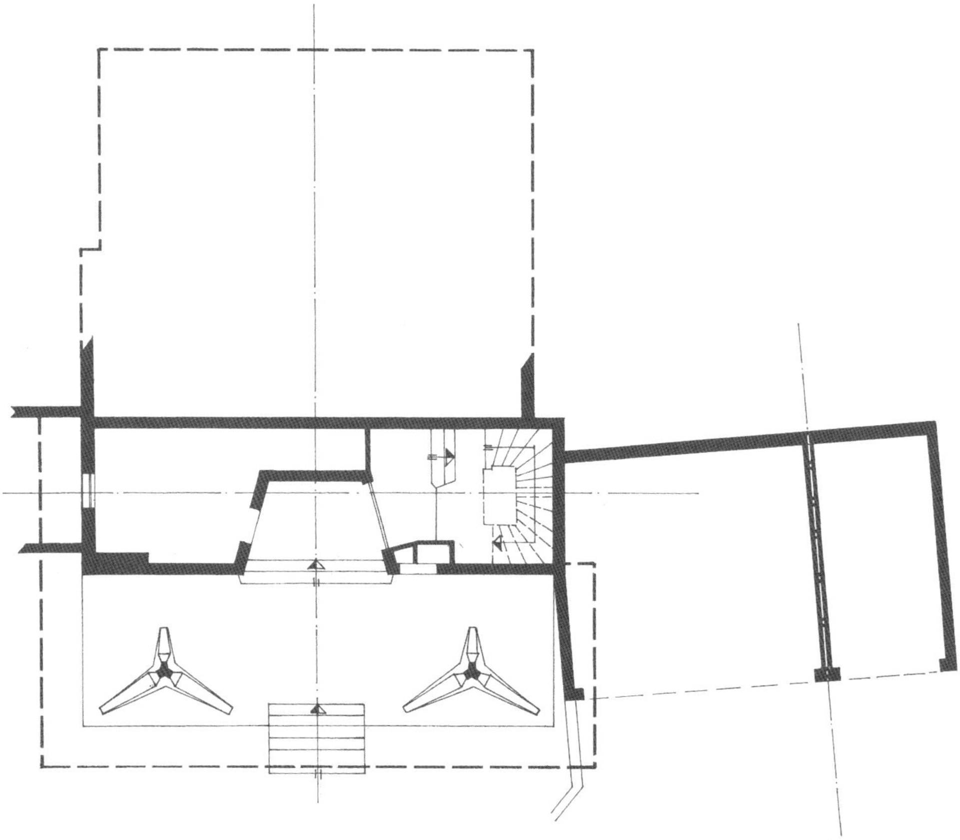

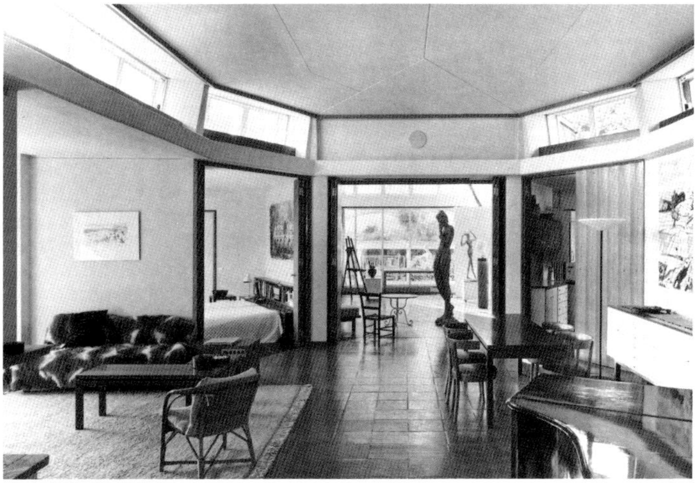

1:200

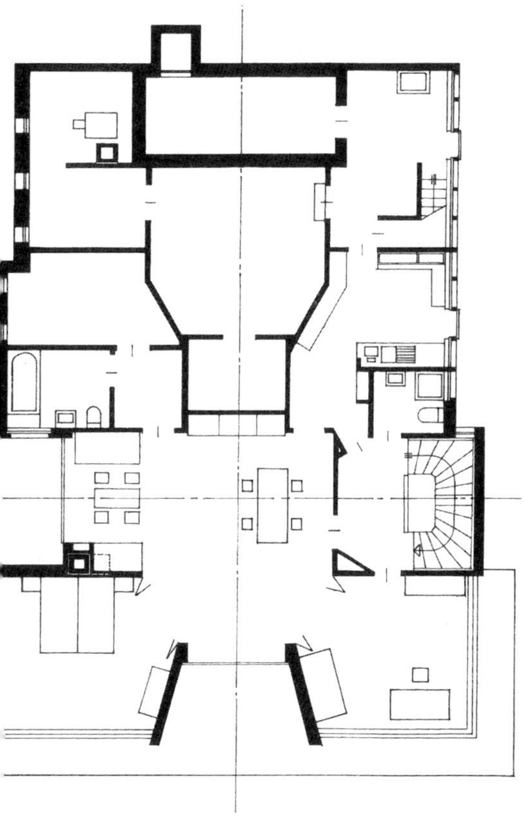

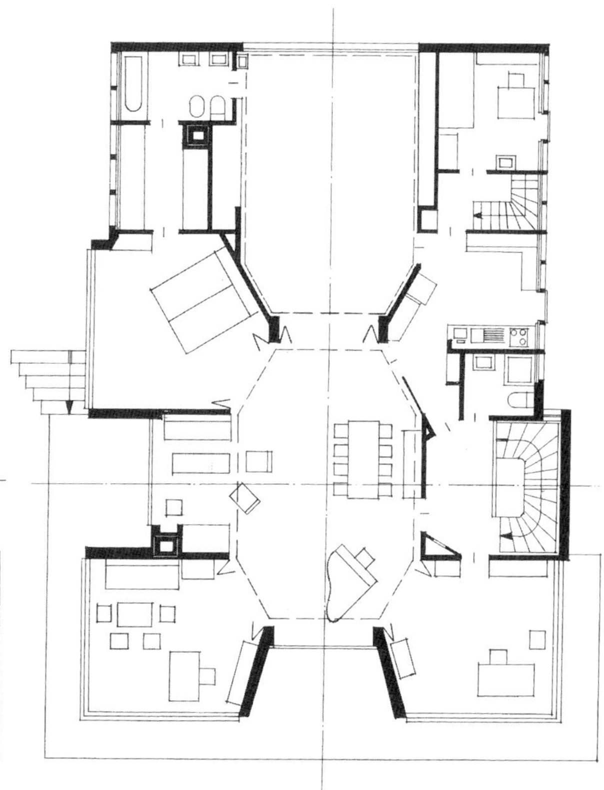

E

Fellowship Home

Alfred Roth

1961

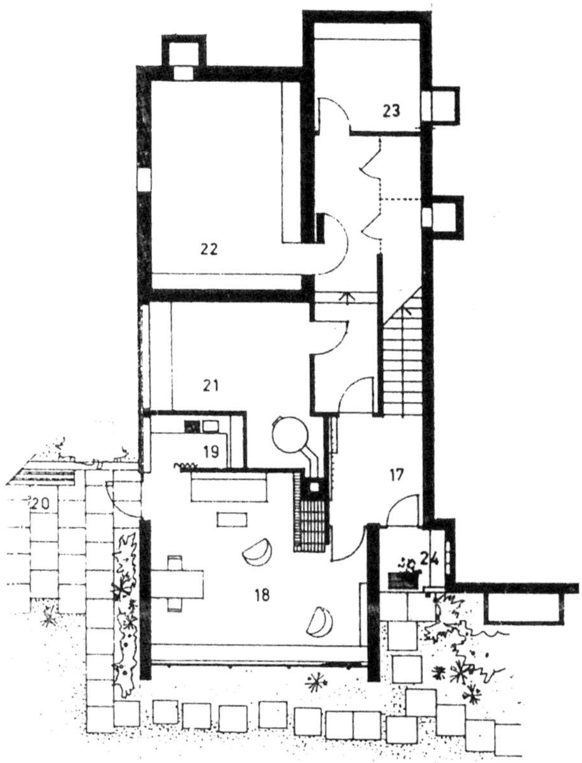

1:200

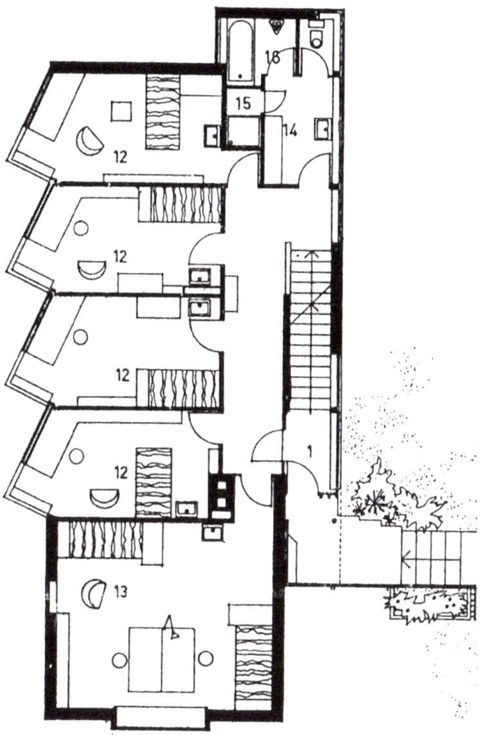

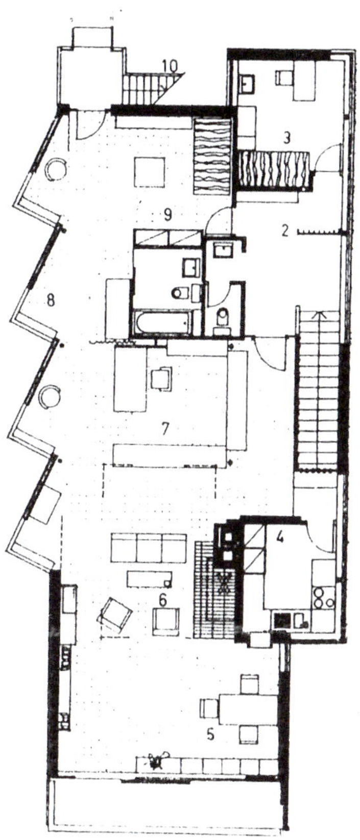

F

Liesch House

Andres Liesch

1971

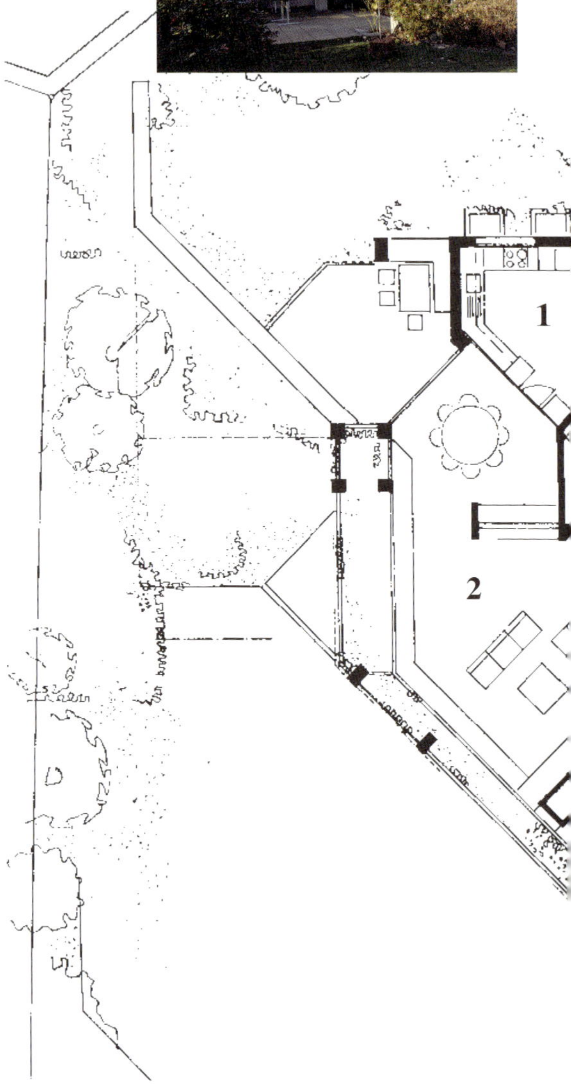

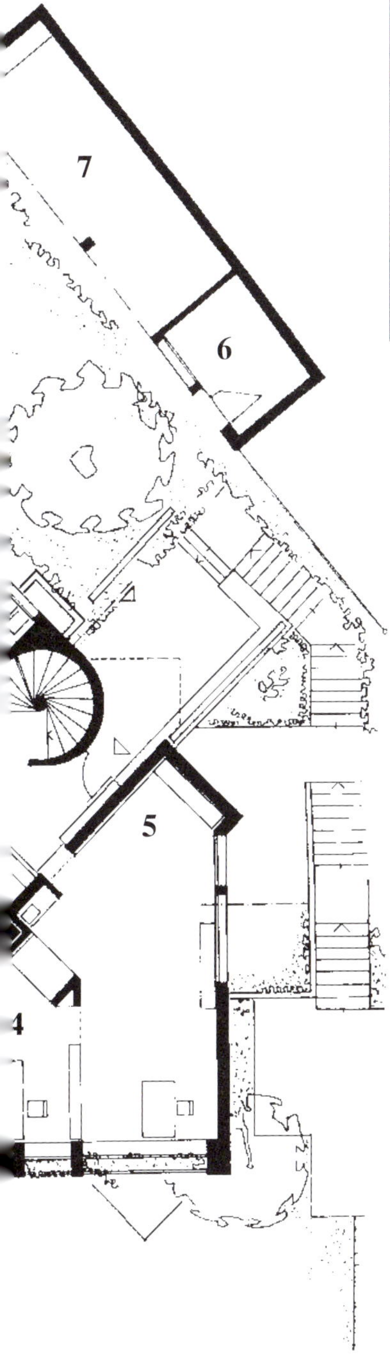

1:200

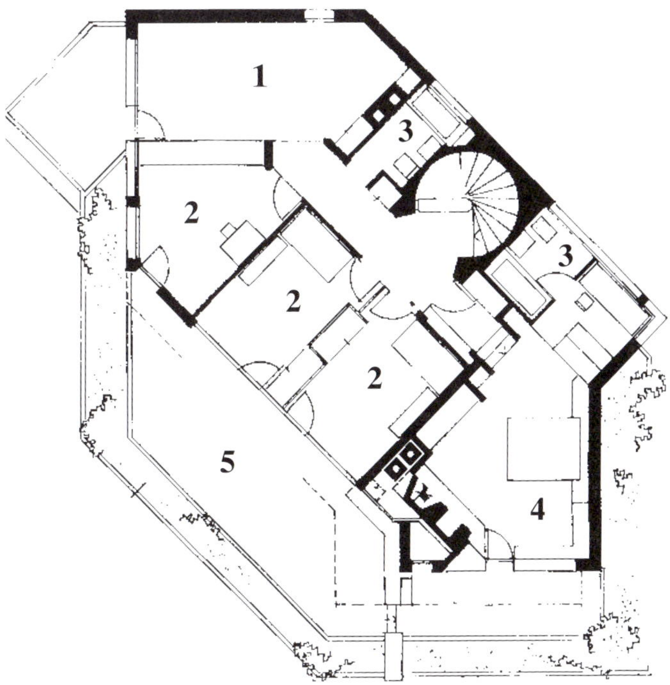

Flora Steiger-Crawford and Rudolf Steiger, circa 1925

998-M

Architects

Flora Steiger-Crawford (1899–1991) **and Rudolf Steiger** (1900–1982)

Flora Steiger-Crawford and Rudolf Steiger studied together at ETH Zurich under Karl Moser. Flora Steiger-Crawford was the first female architect to graduate from ETH. They are two distinctive characters with contrasting biographies.[66]

The Zett House in Zurich (1929–1931)

The Zett House was the first and most significant large-scale modernist urban intervention in Zurich Aussersihl, comparable to the contemporaneous Suva House in Bern by Otto Rudolf Salvisberg or the Schocken department store in Chemnitz (1929–1930) by Erich Mendelsohn. Overlooking the Stauffacher junction, the non-load-bearing facade, executed as a tensioned membrane above the glazed, two-story plinth section, connects Badenerstrasse with Bäckerstrasse. Carl Hubacher was the engineer; his father was the client. There are open-air film screenings in the courtyard.

Flora Steiger-Crawford designed the residential building to the rear on the corner of Rebgasse and Müllergasse with a duplex restaurant and a bar. She likewise created the famous stacking chair based on flat iron bars. This soon became an internationally renowned icon of Swiss design.

General Motors in Biel/Bienne (1935–1936)

The commission came about thanks to Flora Steiger-Crawford's family connection with the client Jean Mussard, who acted as an intermediary between the city and General Motors, and was Flora Steiger-Crawford's brother-in-law. She was not involved in the project, or at least is not mentioned. She was however involved in the project for a detached house for Mussard (1935–1937), although the project was not implemented.

In 1935, General Motors decided to move to Biel/Bienne. One year later, the first car left the assembly line, an incredible achievement. The project was hugely important economically. "Car assembly plant creates jobs throughout the country" was the slogan accompanying one illustration. Engineer Carl Hubacher developed the production hall's striking, wide-span roof construction.

Building signage: Binia Bill

66 — See on this point: Flora Steiger Crawford 2003; Peter Steiger, *Fliegende Möbel und andere Geschichten*, Syntagma Verlag, Freiburg i.B., 2011.

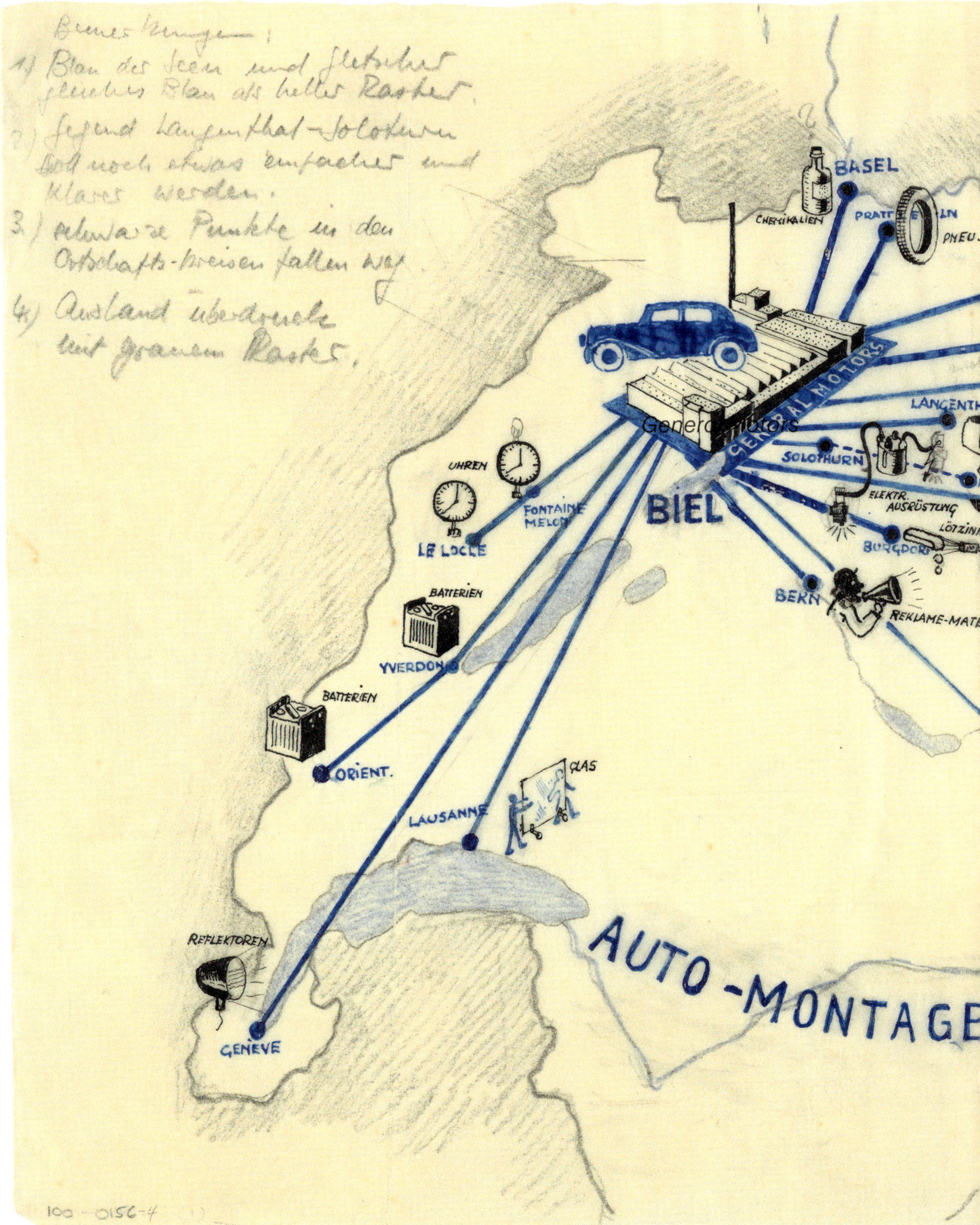
Bemerkungen:
1) Blau der Seen und Gletscher gleiches Blau als heller Raster.
2) Gegend Langenthal-Solothurn soll noch etwas einfacher und klarer werden.
3) schwarze Punkte in den Ortschafts-kreisen fallen weg.
4) Ausland überdrucken mit grauem Raster.
BASEL
CHEMIKALIEN
PNEU.
GENERAL MOTORS
General Motors
SOLOTHURN
ELEKTR. AUSRÜSTUNG
BIEL
UHREN
LE LOCLE
BATTERIEN
YVERDON
BATTERIEN
ORIENT.
BERN
GLAS
LAUSANNE
REFLEKTOREN
GENEVE
AUTO-MONTAGE
100-0156-4

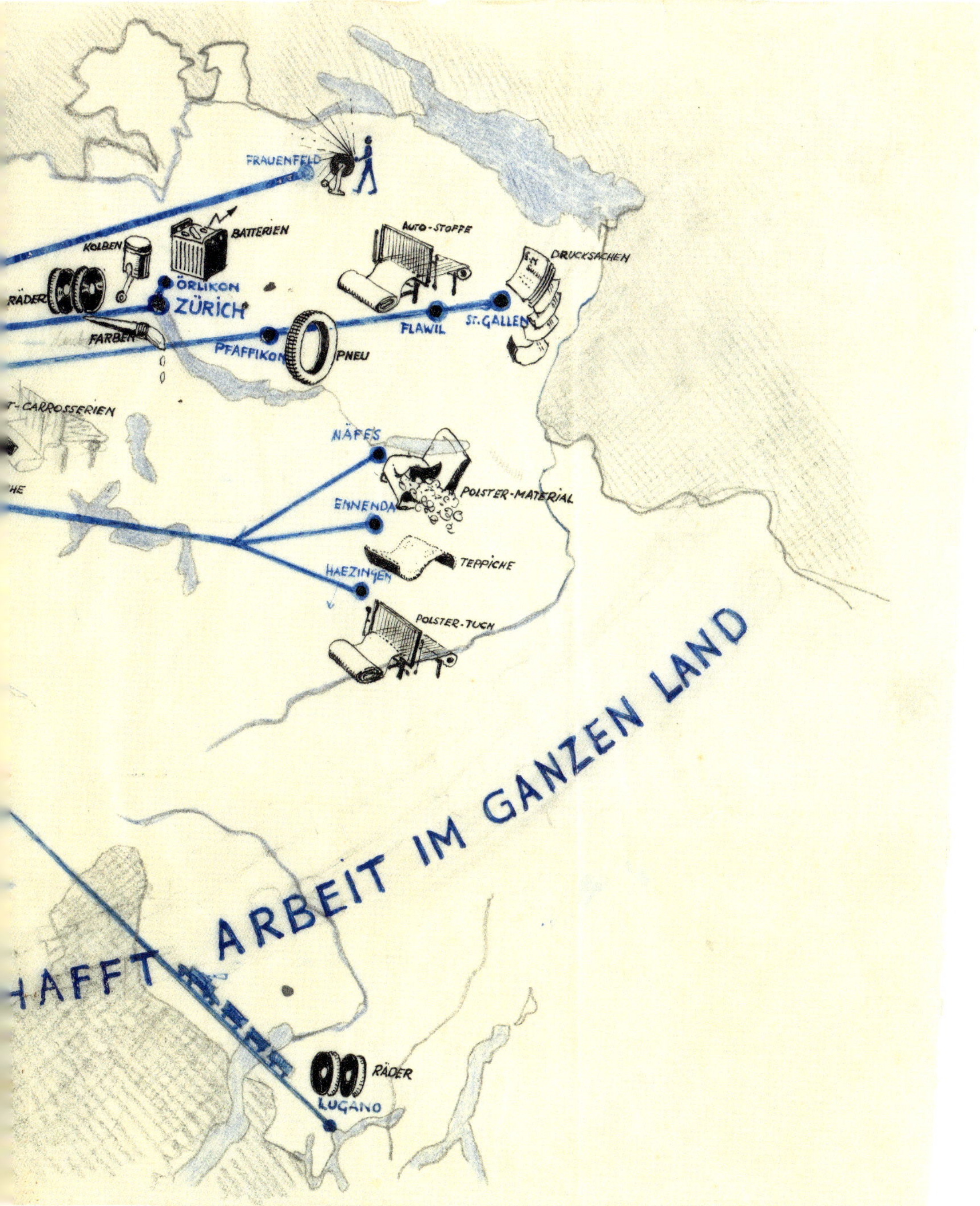
FRAUENFELD
BATTERIEN
KOLBEN
AUTO-STOFFE
DRUCKSACHEN
RÄDER
ÖRLIKON
ZÜRICH
FLAWIL
ST. GALLEN
FARBEN
PFÄFFIKON
PNEU
T-CARROSSERIEN
NÄFELS
POLSTER-MATERIAL
ENNENDA
TEPPICHE
HAEZINGEN
POLSTER-TUCH
HAFFT ARBEIT IM GANZEN LAND
RÄDER
LUGANO

Rudolf Steiger (1900–1982) and Peter Steiger (1928–2023)

CERN (European Council for Nuclear Research) Main Building, Geneva (1958–1960)

One of the major projects on which Rudolf Steiger and his son Peter Steiger cooperated is the main building ensemble for CERN, the European Council for Nuclear Research (Conseil européen pour la recherche nucléaire), in Geneva, which at the time boasted the world's largest particle accelerator. As one of Switzerland's most prestigious research facilities, it was subsequently repeatedly expanded. A new particle accelerator with a 27-kilometer circumference has been added to the original version, which had a diameter of 200 meters and a circumference of 628 meters. A further particle accelerator, the Future Circular Collider, with a circumference of close to 100 km is in the planning stage. As well as being the largest in the world, it will extend across international borders. When the two architects were awarded the contract for the main building, Swiss physicist Paul Scherrer (1890–1969) served as intermediary.

Flora Steiger-Crawford (1899–1991)

The contrast between the sculptures[67] by Flora Steiger-Crawford in the Steiger House, presented in a mise-en-scène by Michel Zumbrunn in 1993, and the circular particle accelerator at the CERN nuclear research main building by Rudolf and Peter Steiger points to the different interests of the spouses. Flora Steiger-Crawford concentrated almost exclusively on sculptural work after 1939.

67 The figures are often slightly oversized, especially due to the distortion of the legs and neck. This means that they do not represent the person sitting for the work, the model, 1:1. The figure "takes on a life of its own" to a certain extent and thus becomes a sculpture.

Leonardo Finotti

Constructed Images

Space and Surface – Reduction to the Two-dimensional

The image becomes a surface yet is nevertheless a spatial paradox; the image space has to be worked out, conceived. Foreground, middle ground and background are set within one plane; everything becomes a surface.

The Unshakable Image – Outline and Vector Framework

The images have their own "inner tension" and are therefore unshakable. The outlines, or rather the silhouettes of the image as a whole, are tensed upon an inner, invisible vector framework in the sense of Rudolf Arnheim's Gestalt theory. [68] To some extent, the sense of depth within the image is abandoned in favor of a two-dimensional figure, as for instance in Le Corbusier's Purist paintings, deploying what is known as the "contour commun" (shared contour line). [69]

Axes as Ordering Lines – Stabilize

Finotti often positions several elements of a photograph in alignment, set "along a line." This creates vertical axes that stabilize the image as an ordering grid pattern and divide it into "nature" and "house" for instance.

Vanishing Lines and Cornerstones – Unfurl

The central perspective is a "means to an end." The vanishing lines are the focus of attention. These end in the corners of the image and "unfurl" it.

Direction and Counter Direction – Mirror

The photos along the same visual axis in opposite directions situate the building between the two vanishing points.

Drone Shots – Parallelisms and Shifts, Abstraction

Systematic "scholarly aerial photographs" capture the ensemble's geometric structure or how the house relates to the garden. With their systematic approach, they reference examples of Concrete Painting by Paul Lohse or Max Bill.

68 Cf. Rudolf Arnheim, *Art and Visual Perception. A Psychology of the Creative Eye*, Berkeley et al., University of California Press, 1954.

69 Cf. Sumi, 1989, p. 102 ff.

View overlooking the Dolder valley towards Lake Zurich.

Biographies

Dieter Kienast

Dieter Kienast (1945–1998) was born in Zurich, where he completed a gardening apprenticeship. He studied landscape planning at the Gesamthochschule Kassel (Kassel University) and completed his doctorate with a thesis on plant sociology. Dieter Kienast taught at the Interkantonales Technikum Rapperswil (Rapperswil Intercantonal Technical College) and ETH Zurich, and was head of the Institut für Landschaft und Garten (Landscape Architecture Department) at Karlsruhe University. From 1979 to 1994, he was co-owner of the planning office Stöckli, Kienast & Koeppel Landschaftsarchitekten. In 1995, he founded Kienast Vogt & Partner Landschaftsarchitekten in Zurich with Günther Vogt.

Lukas Ingold

Lukas Ingold (*1985) completed an apprenticeship as an architectural draftsman and subsequently studied architecture at Bern University of Applied Sciences and ETH Zurich. He completed his doctorate under Prof. Dr. Joseph Schwartz at ETH Zurich, where he also worked as lecturer and led several research projects. He has worked in various architecture firms, including with Christian Kerez in Zurich. He has run his own Zurich-based architecture office since 2014.

Joseph Schwartz

Joseph Schwartz (*1957) studied at the Department of Civil Engineering at ETH Zurich, where he completed his doctorate with a thesis on the design of masonry walls and reinforced concrete columns under normal loads, which was awarded the ETH Silver Medal. He taught at various Swiss universities of applied sciences and was full professor of structural design in the Department of Architecture at ETH Zurich. As co-owner of an engineering office in Zug, Joseph Schwartz was responsible for the planning and execution of various bridge and building construction projects. Since 2002, he has run his own engineering office based in Zug and works closely with several leading Swiss architects.

Arthur Rüegg

Arthur Rüegg (*1942) worked in Zurich, Paris and Boston after studying architecture at ETH Zurich. He taught at ETH Zurich as a full professor of architecture and building construction, and has worked as an architect in Zurich since 1971. Developing models for building within existing structures and persuasive preservation of iconic architecture (such as the Doldertal houses in Zurich) have long numbered among his interests. As part of his intensive research, publication, and exhibition activities on structural design, color, photography, design, and the domestic culture of modernism, he has published numerous monographs and co-curated various exhibitions.

Marianne Burkhalter

Marianne Burkhalter (*1947) completed an apprenticeship as an architectural draftswoman, worked as an architect in Florence (Superstudio), New York, and Los Angeles (Studio Works) and was a visiting student at the University of Princeton. She has taught at the Southern California Institute of Architecture (SCI-ARC) in Los Angeles and at Lausanne's federal institute of technology, the École Polytechnique Fédérale de Lausanne (EPFL).

Christian Sumi

Christian Sumi (*1950) studied at ETH Zurich, where he worked for the Institut für Geschichte und Theorie der Architektur (Institute for the History and Theory of Architecture) (gta). He has taught at the Harvard Graduate School of Design, at EPFL Lausanne, and the University of Strathclyde in Glasgow. Christian Sumi is the author of *Investigations on the Legendary Citroën DS. The Goddess – La Déesse,* published by Lars Müller Publishers in 2020.

Burkhalter Sumi

Marianne Burkhalter and Christian Sumi founded *burkhalter sumi architekten* in 1984. The firm has built up an international reputation, inter alia for its innovative wooden architecture and distinctive polychrome palette. From 2008 to 2016, they held a joint full professorship at the Accademia di Architettura Mendrisio (Academy of Architecture in Mendrisio) (AAM) and founded their own studio in 2020. Marianne Burkhalter and Christian Sumi were awarded the Prix Meret Oppenheim in 2024.[70]

70

Monographs:

Burkhalter Sumi Architects. Projects 2002–2015, Electa, Milan, 2016

"Burkhalter Sumi. Obra reciente / Recent work," in: *2G*, 35, texts by Steven Spier, Barcelona, 2005.

Marianne Burkhalter + Christian Sumi, ed. Heinrich Helfenstein, Princeton Architectural Press, New York, 1999.

Marianne Burkhalter & Christian Sumi – Die Holzbauten, Zurich, gta Verlag, 1995.

Publications:

Der Gotthard. Il Gottardo. Landscape. Myths. Technology, eds. Marianne Burkhalter, Christian Sumi, Zurich, Scheidegger und Spiess, 2016.

Konrad Wachsmann and the Grapevine Structure, eds. Marianne Burkhalter, Christian Sumi, Zurich, Park Books, 2018.

Chronology

	Architect Flora Steiger-Crawford and Rudolf Steiger
1959	Completion of the Steiger House
1970	Extension to upper apartment, first plans as early as 1958
1971	Extension, adding pergola to upper apartment
1980	Installation of elevator in stairwell

	Architect Hansruedi Meier
1991	Complete refurbishment

	Architects Gret Loewensberg, Marianne Burkhalter, Christian Sumi
1993	Conversion of the laundry room in the lower apartment into a bedroom, direct access to the sculpture cellar
1997	Roof renovation
2007	Installation of a library in the lower apartment in the former sculpture cellar
2010	New kitchen in lower apartment
2011	New kitchen in upper apartment
2023	Renovation of skylight in upper apartment

	Landscape architect Dieter Kienast
1993	Redesign of the garden

Steiger House, Bergstrasse 67, 8032 Zurich

Acknowledgments

We would especially like to thank Peter Steiger. He provided us with the comprehensive plans for the building (now in the gta Archives of ETH Zurich). They form the basis of this publication.

We thank the publisher, Lars Müller, for all the inspiring conversations, and the project coordinator Emilia Maier. A special thanks goes to the gta Archives of ETH Zurich, to Irina Devidoivi; to Almut Grunewald and Danielle Weiss for their helpful research in the archives; and to Ulrike Steiner from the gta Verlag at ETH Zurich.

We thank Karin Schiesser for the graphic design of the book; Hansruedi Meier for the current plan materials; Fabrizio Rocchè, Jonas Hertig and Morris Blaser for the image processing; and Simone Biaggi and Tuja Gianesi for further archival information.

We would like to thank Dieter Kienast, Josef Schwartz, Lukas Ingold and Arthur Rüegg for their contributions to the book.

Our thanks also goes out to the photographers Michel Zumbrunn, Georg Aerni, and especially to Leonardo Finotti. His photographs form the backbone of this publication and situate the house in the present day.

Finally, a big thank you goes to Belacqua Immobilien AG, Herrliberg. Marianne Burkhalter and Christian Sumi, the editors, are very pleased about the generous support.

Credits

Bibliografie

"Architect's Own House", *Architectural Design*, 9, 1962, pp. 419–420.

Rudolf Steiger, "Haus Steiger an der Bergstrasse in Zürich," *Schweizerische Bauzeitung* 81, 33, 1963, pp. 590–591, plates 39–41.

Rudolf Steiger, *46 Jahre Bauen + Planen in Zürich*, 1970, p. 127–130.

Haefeli Moser Steiger, *Archithese* 10, 2, 1980.

Irene Meier, "Designer Möbel im Steiger–Haus," *Ideales Heim*, January 1993, pp.36–45

Flora Steiger-Crawford (1899–1991), ed. ETH Zurich, gta Verlag, Zurich, 2003.

Haefeli Moser Steiger. Die Architekten der Schweizer Moderne, eds. Sonja Hildebrand, Bruno Maurer, Werner Oechslin,exh. cat. Museum für Gestaltung, Zurich, gta Verlag, 2007.

Peter Steiger, *Chancen und Widerstände auf dem Weg zum nachhaltigen Planen und Bauen*, Zürich, gta Verlag, 2009.

Peter Steiger, *Fliegende Möbel und andere Geschichten*, Freiburg, Syntagma, 2011.

Text Credits

20-26: excerpt from Dieter Kienast, Gärten. Gardens, Birkhäuser Verlag, Basel, 1997, 146-148.
Translation by Bruce Almbern and Katja Steiner / Kienast/Vogt Partners.

Image Credits and Sources

(l) = left, (r) = right, (t) = top, (b) = bottom, (m) = middle

Photographs

Cover, 8–9, 11, 13, 14–19, 21, 22–25, 31 (b), 68–75, 85 (r), 96, 129, 132–133, 136–137, 183, 184–185: Leonardo Finotti

28–29: Georg Aerni

31(t), 93,168,169,170: Fotografie: Walter Binder, courtesy of gta Archiv/ETH Zurich / Haefeli Moser Steiger

31 (mt): Rasmus Norlander

31 (b): Craig Ellwood / source: Esther McCoy, *Craig Ellwood Architecture*, Alfieri, Venice, 1968

85 (l), 181 (t): gta Archiv/ETH Zürich / Peter Steiger

86–91, 108–111, 120, 181 (b): Michel Zumbrunn

117 (t), 125, 127, 141–147, 149: Karin Schiesser

117 (b), 118, 149 (tl): Christian Sumi

150–151: photographs: Dolf Hüppi, courtesy of Fotostiftung Schweiz, Winterthur

155, 164: source: Peter Meyer, *Moderne Schweizer Wohnhäuser*, Zurich, 1928.

162: source: *Schweizerische Bauzeitung*, 71/72, 3, 1918

166: photographs: Hans Staub, courtesy of gta Archiv/ETH Zurich / Alfred Roth

167, 171: photographs: Hans Finsler, 2024 Familie Lips©, courtesy of gta Archiv/ETH Zurich / Alfred Roth

172–173: photographs: Heinrich Helfenstein©, courtesy of gta Archiv/ETH Zurich

174–175: gta Archiv/ETH Zurich / Flora Steiger-Crawford and Rudolf Steiger

177 (tl, ml): gta Archiv/ETH Zurich / Grete Hubacher-Knokke and Karl Hubacher

177 (br): Franz Xaver Jaggy, Museum für Gestaltung Zürich, Designsammlung, ZHdK

Plans and Drawings

Cover: Jonas Hertig, Moritz Morris

27: source: Dieter Kienast, *Gärten. Gardens*, Birkhäuser Verlag, Basel, 1997, 146-148. / Kienast/Vogt Partners

33–41, 43–61, 84–85, 98–107, 114–127, 130–131, 134–135, 138–139, 168–169, 178–179: gta Archiv/ETH Zurich / Haefeli Moser Steiger

62–67, 80 (r): Hansruedi Meier Architekturbüro Zurich

76–77: courtesy of Gio Ponti Archives

79, 81 (b): source: Giacomo Scamozzi, *L'idea dell architettura universale*, Venice, 1615, Public Domain

80 (l), 130: Rudolf Steiger, *46 Jahre Bauen und Planen*, Zurich, 1970.

81 (t): source: *Andrea Palladio, I quatro libri dell'architettura*, Venice, 1570, Public Domain

83 (t): Esch Sintzel Architekten Zürich

83 (t): EMI Architekt*innen Zürich

153: source: Arthur Rüegg, *Die Doldertalhäuser 1932–1936. Ein Hauptwerk des Neuen Bauens in Zürich*, gta Verlag, Zurich, 1996

163: source: *Schweizerische Bauzeitung*, 71/72, 3, 1918

165: source: Peter Meyer, *Moderne Schweizer Wohnhäuser*, Zurich, 1928

166–167, 170–171: gta Archiv/ETH Zurich / Alfred Roth

172–173: source: *Das Ideale Heim*, February 2012

Imprint

The Steiger House
Doldertal, Zurich 1959
Rudolf Steiger and Flora-Steiger Crawford

Authors: Marianne Burkhalter and Christian Sumi
Texts by: Dieter Kienast, Arthur Rüegg, Joseph Schwartz and Lukas Ingold
Translation: Helen Ferguson
Copyediting (German): Viola van Beek
Proofreading: Stephanie Shellabear
Photography: Leonardo Finotti
Project coordination: Emilia Maier
Design: Karin Schiesser
Graphic post-processing plans: Fabrizio Rocchè, Karin Schiesser
Lithography: Gundula Seraphin, Bad Münstereifel, Germany
Printing and binding: Graspo, Zlín, the Czech Republic
Paper: GardaPat 13, Bianka, 135 g/qm

Lars Müller Publishers
Zurich, Switzerland
www.lars-mueller-publishers.com

ISBN 978-3-03778-767-0

Distributed in North America, Latin America and the Caribbean by ARTBOOK | D.A.P.
www.artbook.com

Printed in the Czech Republic